EVERY SCHOOL

EVERY SCHOOL

ONE CITIZEN'S GUIDE TO

TRANSFORMING EDUCATION

DONALD P. NIELSEN

SEATTLE   DISCOVERY INSTITUTE PRESS   2014

Description

How would an entrepreneur reform education? In *Every School*, Don Nielsen draws on his business career and two decades as a school activist, to offer innovative solutions to the educational challenges facing our country. Lasting change, Nielsen argues, will not come mainly through local school boards, but rather through state legislative action that empowers school administrators to make choices in the interests of their students. The book is essential reading for parents, policymakers and citizens who want to improve the present system, and who have the courage to pursue the recommendations contained within.

Library Cataloging Data

Every School: One Citizen's Guide to Transforming Education by Donald P. Nielsen

216 pages, 6 x 9 x 0.5 inches & 0.7 lb, 229 x 152 x 12 mm. & 0.30 kg

Library of Congress Control Number: 2014951118

ISBN-13 978-1-936599-21-9 (paperback)

BISAC: EDU034000 Education/Educational Policy & Reform/General

BISAC: EDU000000 Education/General

BISAC: EDU001020 Education/Administration/Elementary & Secondary

Publisher Information

Discovery Institute Press, 208 Columbia Street, Seattle, WA 98104

Internet: http://www.discoveryinstitutepress.com/

Published in the United States of America on acid-free paper.

First Edition, First Printing., September 2014.

To the thousands of teachers and principals who
achieve amazing results in spite of the system.

And to my wife, Melissa, for tolerating my passion for public
education and for being such a wonderful partner for 54 years.

Advanced Praise for *Every School*

"Don Nielsen provides unusually clear insight into the complex issues that inhibit high educational attainment of our public school systems. He follows up the diagnosis with a series of feasible and practical recommendations for how to improve our schools. Nielsen's book should be a must-read for anyone interested in public education."

—ALLEN S. GROSSMAN, SENIOR FELLOW, MBA CLASS OF 1957, PROFESSOR OF MANAGEMENT PRACTICE RETIRED, HARVARD BUSINESS SCHOOL

"In what seems to be a reoccurring challenge with each generation, the question remains how we can best address our nation's deficiencies in our K–12 educational system. It is a question that must be answered if we are to achieve our highest potential as a nation and in our children. Don Nielsen provides a thoughtful response. He not only addresses the root causes of our challenges, but provides a framework for how to align P-12 education to achieve greater effectiveness and results—corporately and individually. Don's background as co-founder, President, and Chairman of Hazleton Corporation and as the former President of the Board for the Seattle Public Schools provides a unique and grounded perspective to the solutions he offers."

—DAN MARTIN, PHD, PRESIDENT, SEATTLE PACIFIC UNIVERSITY

"This is an important book—insightful, engaging and anchored in the real problems and opportunities that communities face. Educators, community leaders, and policymakers are fortunate that Don Nielsen has turned his attention and talent to this analysis of contemporary schooling and what we need to do to harness its potential to create responsible citizens. Don is uniquely suited for this role—a community leader, businessman, parent, chair of a large city school board, and informed citizen. The book is practical and revolutionary at the same time and should be on anyone's required reading list if they care about the future of public education."

—ROBERT C. PIANTA, PH.D., DEAN, CURRY SCHOOL OF EDUCATION, UNIVERSITY OF VIRGINIA

CONTENTS

PREFACE

Horace Mann, who is considered the father of our public schools, established America's public education system in the mid-nineteenth century. Prior to the common school, most children were either schooled at home or in small village schools. The level of education of a child really depended upon the effort and desire of the parents. Families and the communities they lived in took on the responsibility of educating children.

Parents had a wide variety of education options including extensive home schooling. Other options included: "private benevolent associations, private-venture schools, Latin grammar schools, religious schools, boarding schools and private academies."[1] These early schools did a pretty good job of educating children.

Hamilton was twenty in the retreat from New York, Burr, was twenty-one; Light Horse Harry Lee, twenty-one; Lafayette, nineteen. What amounted to a college class rose up and struck down the British Empire, afterwards helping to write the most sophisticated governing documents in modern history.[2]

George Washington had no schooling until he was eleven, no classroom confinement, no blackboards. He arrived at school already knowing how to read, write and calculate about as well as the average college student today.[3]

In 1837, Mann was appointed to be the first Secretary of Education for the state of Massachusetts. In that office, he set about to establish a

---

1. Terry M. Moe, editor, *A Primer on America's Schools* (Stanford: Hoover Institution Press, 2001), 5-6.
2. John Taylor Gatto, *The Underground History of American Education* (New York: Oxford Village Press, 1995), 25.
3. Ibid., 31.

system of schools for his state. He felt that all children should receive a good education. While in office, he traveled to Europe to study school systems there. In Prussia (now a part of Germany), he found what he was looking for. King Fredrick the Great of Prussia had set up a system of tax-supported schools designed to provide an eight-year course of compulsory education to all children. The Prussian schools provided not only the skills needed in an early industrialized world, (reading writing and arithmetic), but also provided a strict education in ethics, duty, discipline and obedience.

> Focusing on following directions, basic skills, and conformity, he [King Frederick] sought to indoctrinate the nation from an early age. Isolating students in rows and teachers in individual classrooms fashioned in strict hierarchy—intentionally fostering fear and loneliness.[4]

> Mann chose the Prussian model, with its depersonalized learning and strict hierarchy of power, because it was the cheapest and easiest way to teach literacy on a large scale.[5]

> Massachusetts adopted this system and became the first state to provide all of its citizens access to a free public education. Over the next 66 years, every other state made the same guarantee. The result was a publicly-funded system where, in every American classroom, groups of about 28 students of roughly the same age are taught by one teacher, usually in an 800 square-foot room. This model has been the dominant archetype ever since.[6]

Early in the twentieth century, all states had adopted compulsory education (each new state added to the union enacted similar laws) and had combined that with child labor laws that prevented children from being hired for factory employment.

---

4. New American Academy, "The Prussian-Industrial Model: The Roots of Modern Public Schooling," at webpage http://thenewamericanacademy.org/index.php/home/our-philosophy-menu/the-prussian-industrial-model.

5. Ibid.

6. Joel Rose, "How to Break Free of Our 19th Century Factory-Model Education System," *The Atlantic* (May 19, 2012), http://www.theatlantic.com/business/archive/2012/05/how-to-break-free-of-our-19th-century-factory-model-education-system/256881/.

In his 1919 *Public Education in the United States*, Ellwood P. Cubberley suggested that modern life had deprived children of the training that life in farms and villages had once provided, so public schools must take up the task of preparing them for industry and society.[7]

As the country grew, and immigrants began to flood this nation, school populations dramatically increased. The Great Depression caused another major increase in school attendance.

> The 1920's provided the initial burst in high school attendance, but the Great Depression added significantly to high school enrollment and graduation rates.[8]

High school, not college, was the predominate educational attainment during the first half of the twentieth century. Increased high school graduation rates created a work force ideal for the manufacturing boom that was occurring. A school system that treated students like raw material and treated them to a uniform education created a workforce perfectly designed for the production line job. However, "as late as 1950, only 25 percent of black students and 50 percent of white students remained in high school long enough to earn a diploma."[9]

The original Prussian school system selected a few students to go onto higher education with the balance being educated to a level that would allow them to work in the factories or on the farm. Our school system did the same.

The factory model of education is still with us today. That model was, and still is, designed to effectively educate all children to a certain level and allow a few to rise to advanced levels. Today, as in decades past, our schools effectively educate about 25 percent of our students, another 50 percent graduate with limited skills that do not prepare them for the world of work, and 20–25 percent drop out prior to graduation. This

---

7. Ellwood P. Cubberly, *Public Education in the United States* (Boston: Houghton-Mifflin, 1919), 355.

8. Claudia Goldin, "How America Graduated From High School, 1910–1960, National Bureau of Economic Research, June 1994.

9. Thomas Toch, *In the Name of Excellence* (New York: Oxford University Press, 1991), 3.

has been the case for decades. I would argue that this performance is designed into the system and we cannot change the outcome without changing the system.

Prior to the early 1960s, this type of performance was acceptable. Our economy was largely a manufacturing economy and those who entered the work force needed only a rudimentary level of reading, writing and mathematical skills. In the first half of the twentieth century, except during the Depression, a person with limited skills could still find a living wage job, could buy a house, and raise a family. In fact, in my high school class of 1956, a majority of my peers did not go on to college, but rather went into the job market and most have lived a very comfortable life.

That environment started to change in the late Fifties and early Sixties. Manufacturing started to decline and the service economy started to expand. Over the next fifty years, we have seen our economy move from being manufacturing-based, to information- and service-based and recently, I would argue that we are moving into an Internet-driven economy as businesses can literally become a global enterprise from the get go. As this occurred, the skills and education needed in the American job has dramatically increased.

Numerous other changes in our society have occurred that have impacted our schools. Those are delineated in Chapter 2, but suffice to say, today's society is totally different from what I faced when I graduated from high school and the demands on the educational proficiency of children has also changed.

However, during this half century, our schools have operated much as they have always done even though there have been literally hundreds of reform efforts attempted. What we have witnessed is an institution that is very resistant to change.

Students continue to attend school for six hours per day for approximately 180 days per year. Within schools the curriculum and schedule continue to resemble that which was prevalent in the first half of the twentieth century. In fact, high school graduation requirements remain largely unchanged. Someone once said, "If Rip Van Winkle had gone to sleep January 1, 1900 and woke up on January 1, 2000, the only aspect of our society that would be familiar would be the school." That's probably correct. But if our schools are, as I believe, the most important institution in our society, it goes without saying that they must not only keep up with the changes in our society, but anticipate the future. Our schools do none of that.

Failing to adjust to societal changes has caused our schools to educate poorly or to under-educate almost three generations of our citizens. The impact of this failure is readily seen in the children now coming into our schools. Poorly educated adults are more likely to live in poverty. Their lifetime income will be a third that of a college graduate. Children raised in poverty are the least prepared for learning. Today, most public school systems, particularly in urban areas, have a disproportionate number of children raised in poverty. In fact, "Researchers report that low-income students are now a majority in the public schools of the U.S. South, and that schools in the West may cross the line in the near future. As a nation, all public schools average 46 percent of their students coming from families living in poverty."[10] Harold Hodgkinson, an Alexandria, Virginia-based education demographer states that the U.S. now has the highest percentage of children living in poverty of any of the 24 Organization for Economic Cooperation and Development member nations. The U.S. has held that distinction for more than 10 years.[11]

This is occurring even after the "War on Poverty" that was established in 1964 during the presidency of Lyndon Johnson. At that time, the country had 16 percent of its citizens living in poverty. Today, after more than $15 trillion of expenditures to eliminate poverty, we have a poverty rate of 17 percent and growing.

---

10. "Eye on Research," *Education Week* (November 7, 2007), 14.

11. Harold L. Hodgkinson, quoted in Debra Viadero, "South's Schools Pass Milestone on Poverty," *Education Week* (November 7, 2007), 14.

This increase in poverty is a direct reflection of the failure of our public schools to effectively educate the nation's children. As the demands for education increased, and our schools failed to adjust, the net effect has become an ever-increasing percentage of under-educated adults.

Unless we improve our schools, we will continue to turn out young adults without the knowledge and skills needed to gain employment in an ever increasingly complex society.

It is based upon that reality that this book is written. In the following pages, I will endeavor to provide a blueprint for the changes needed in our education system and the rationale for each. It is obvious that the country must effectively educate every child and it is equally obvious that we cannot do so with the present system of public education.

The book is divided into three sections; Part One deals with the existing arena of public education, Part Two suggest three specific changes that need to be made before any other changes are likely to work, and Part Three suggests follow on changes that should occur, provided the first three have been implemented.

Part One: The Current Landscape

THE FIRST four chapters look at the current state of our public education system.

Chapter 1 describes the existing system. We will look at how school is set up, how people enter the profession and how learning occurs or fails to occur in public schools.

Chapter 2 describes the external environment in which our public schools operate. This discussion is included because, over the last 70 years our entire society has changed, but our schools are still organized very much the same way. These societal changes have been labeled "External Factors." These factors have impacted our schools, but public school officials have almost no control over any of them. The list of such factors is quite extensive.

Chapter 3 discusses the mission of school. This is a topic, which everyone claims to know, yet when you dig into the subject, you find the reality is quite different. I found no one who could articulate a meaningful mission statement for schools, so I developed my own. Unless everyone agrees on the mission of education, it is impossible to create a system to achieve it.

Chapter 4 discusses unions and change. In this chapter we look at how unions developed, why they are so powerful, how they constrain change and how they can be dealt with in our effort to improve schools.

Part Two: First Steps for Change

THE NEXT three chapters delineate three areas of reform that must be addressed before any other reforms can become sustainable.

Chapter 5 deals with teaching. Here we look at the profession that is the most important in our society, the one from which all others are born and suggest how it needs to change to ensure a quality teacher in every classroom.

Chapter 6 deals with the issue of leadership. If we improve teaching and do not improve leadership, we will fail. So, in this chapter we look at how we now select and train education leaders and describe how we should select and train leaders.

Chapter 7 focuses on governance. If we fix teaching and leadership, but do not address governance, we will not succeed in fixing our schools. Ineffective governance is a roadblock to providing effective education for our children.

Part Three: Next Steps

IN THIS section, we look at additional system changes that should be implemented if the first three are put in place.

Chapter 8 looks at group versus individual education and suggests how we must change the system to cater to the needs of the individual child.

Chapter 9 discusses a longer school day and school year along with the issue of time versus achievement.

Chapter 10 focuses on technology and how it is a "game changer" for education.

Chapter 11 discusses three major reform ideas: choice, vouchers and charter schools.

Chapter 12 takes a look at brain development and early childhood education.

Chapter 13 concludes the book with a call to action.

Making our public schools work for every child is the most important thing we can do for our children and for our country. It is imperative that we deal with this institution now and make the changes needed to fundamentally improve the education provided to our children. I hope this book will play some small role in making that happen. We need excellence in "Every School."

Acknowledgements

For the past 22 years I have been able to speak to and to visit with wonderful people in the fields of education, business, government and unions. So many so that it would be impossible to include everyone. There were, however, some people who were particularly helpful and deserve special thanks.

This whole effort started in 1992 with a phone call to then-Secretary of Education, Lamar Alexander, now the current senior senator from Tennessee. I thank him for seeing me and introducing me to David Kearns who was extraordinarily helpful. David was the former CEO of Xerox and was, when we met, the Assistant Secretary of Education. David started me on a wonderful path of learning that is culminated with this book.

One of my most meaningful encounters was with Betty Wallace, who was then the Superintendent of the Vance County School District in Vance County, N.C. She still is the most profoundly talented educator I have ever met.

Along the way, I was privileged to meet with leaders in all facets of government and education. People like Ernie Boyer, President of the Carnegie Institute, Joel Klein, Chancellor of the New York Public Schools, Michelle Rhee, both at Teach For America and as Superintendent of Schools in Washington, D.C., Don Ingwerson, former Superintendent of the Jefferson County Schools (Louisville, KY), Dr. Martin Eaddy (Superintendent of Lincolnton, N.C., School District), Arlene Ackerman (Superintendent of Philadelphia Schools), Barbara Byrd-Bennett (Superintendent of Cleveland, OH., schools), Susan Enfield (Highline Schools in Washington State), John Fryer (Duvall County

Public Schools in Florida), Richard DeLorenzo (Chugach School System in Anchorage, AL), Alan Bersin (San Diego),Tom Payzant (Boston), Diana Lam (Providence, RI) and Jerome "Jerry" Wartgow (Denver).

I also met with governors; Governor Booth Gardner (Washington), Bob McDonald (Virginia), Mitch Daniels (Indiana), Roy Romer (Colorado, and then Superintendent of Los Angeles Schools) and James Hunt (North Carolina). Jeb Bush read the manuscript and provided helpful suggestions. Others who let me pick their brains on education issues included Rob Paige (Superintendent of Houston Public Schools and then Secretary of Education), Lou Gerstner (former Chairman of IBM and Chair of the Teaching Commission), Ross Perot (while working on education reform in Texas), John Doerr (Partner of Kleiner Perkins and The New Venture Fund), Frank Schrontz and Phil Condit (both former Chairmen of Boeing), Christopher Cross (former Deputy Secretary of Education) and Terry Bergeson (former Superintendent of Public Instruction for Washington State).

School principals were helpful, particularly Marja Brandon, one of the finest educators I have ever known (Seattle Girls School) and Larry Rosenstock (creator of High Tech High in San Diego),

Union leaders also were helpful. I had the privilege of talking with and learning from Keith Geiger (NEA President), Al Shanker (AFT President) Carla Nuxol (President of the Washington State Education Association), Roger Erskine (Executive Director of the Seattle Education Association) and Dal Lawrence from Toledo, OH.

Deans of Education Schools and of Business Schools were of assistance. Those included Kim Clark (Former Dean of the Harvard Business School), Bob Bruner (Dean of the Darden School at the University of Virginia), Bob Pianta (Dean of the Curry School at the University of Virginia), Tom Stritikus and Pat Wasley (current and former deans of the Education School at the University of Washington), Francisco Rios, (Dean of the Education School at the Western Washington University), Brian Burton (Former Dean of the School of Business and Economics at Western Washington University), Kathleen McCartney (Former Dean of the Harvard Graduate School of Education) and the late Sue Schmitt(Former Dean of the School of Education at Seattle University). I can't leave the higher education community without a special thank you to Professor Allen Grossman who was the chief developer of the Public Education Leadership Program (PELP) at the Harvard Business School and to both Dean Robert Pianta and Dean Robert Bruner for their support in developing the dual degree program in education leadership at the University of Virginia. These three gentlemen are true leaders in improving the operational effectiveness of our Country's schools. Others in higher education include; Tony Wagner (Harvard Graduate School of Education), Stig Leschly (Harvard Business School) Tim Garson (former Provost of the University of Virginia), Dan Martin (President of Seattle Pacific University), Bruce Shepard (President of Western Washington University), Father Stephen Sundborg (President of Seattle University), Elson Floyd (President of Washington State University) and Mark Emmert (former President of the University of Washington).

Special thanks goes to the late John Stanford (former Superintendent of Seattle Pubic Schools) who taught me more about the power of leadership than anyone I have ever met and to Joseph Oschefsky who followed John as Superintendent, to several of my colleagues who served with me on the School Board of Seattle Public Schools; notably Ellen Roe, Linda Harris, Barbara Schaad-Lamphere, Al Sugiyama, Dr. Scott Barnhart, Nancy Waldman, Michael Preston, Barbara Petersen, and David Brown

Others, in the Seattle community, who deserve thanks include; Artie Buerk (co-founder of the Alliance for Education), Robin Pasquarella (former President of the Alliance for Education), and Sara Morris (current President of the Alliance for Education). Nearby, in Bellevue, Washington, were the late Mike Riley (former Superintendent of Bellevue Public Schools) and Judy Bushnell (former president of the

Bellevue School Board), one of my mentors on so many education issues. I also want to thank Dr. John Medina who is not only a friend, but was extremely helpful in providing me information for the commentary on brain development.

In the nonprofit world, I benefited from conversations with; John Schur (New Leaders for New Schools), Marc Tucker (president of the National Center for Education and the Economy), Eli Broad (Broad Foundation), Michael Feinberg (KIPP), and Liv Fenne (education director of the Washington Policy Center). From the Gates Foundation, I appreciate my discussions with Tom Vander Ark (former head of their education initiative), Vicki Phillips (director of their education programs), Martha Choe (chief operating officer) and Bill Gates, Sr., who is not only a friend, but read the manuscript and provided some wonderful insights.

I especially want to thank Paul Guppy of the Washington Policy Center, my daughter-in-law, Sandy Nielsen, Kathy Henning of Seattle Pacific University, and Michael W. Perry of Inkling Books for their help in editing the manuscript. I also want to thank my daughter, Kristin Merlo Nielsen, for her assistance in editing this book. Kristin has become as passionate about education as have I, and I greatly value her views and her assistance.

Finally, I want to thank President Steve Brui, Chairman Bruce Chapman, Eric Garcia, Audrey Southgate and Anna Salick of Discovery Institute, for their wise counsel and support in making this book a reality.

Introduction

OVER THE LAST 25 YEARS, I HAVE DEVOTED A GREAT DEAL OF MY time to learn about and participate in the public educational system of our country. From that involvement, I have developed some definite opinions about the system that I hope will help others, especially office holders, parents and private citizens who are concerned about public schools.

My experience and background is as a businessman and entrepreneur. I am not an educator and make no claims to be one. Rather, I am an interested and concerned citizen who has taken a serious look at our public educational system.

In way of background, my wife, Melissa, and I were raised and educated in the State of Washington attending public schools in Seattle. We both graduated from the University of Washington (1960 and 1961) after which we married and moved to Virginia where I completed my six-month active duty tour with the U.S. Army. In 1961, we relocated to Boston where I attended the Harvard Business School, and she taught in a public high school.

After getting my MBA, we returned to Seattle where I went to work for a large, Seattle-based company, and my wife gave birth to the first of our three children.

In 1969, another fellow and I started a company in the basement of an A&P Store. In 1971, we purchased a Virginia-based company, Hazleton Laboratories, Inc.

For the next 23 years, we built that company into a multi-national business that ultimately (1983) listed on the New York Stock Exchange under the name Hazleton Corporation. In 1987, we sold the Company to Corning, Inc. I stayed on to run the company for another five years and retired in 1992.

At 54, I felt too young to fully retire. I had achieved my business goals and wanted to do something radically different with the rest of my life. I picked public education. That choice had many roots. First, I had served on the board of Junior Achievement of Metropolitan Washington for many years and served as chairman for three years. I also was a member of the Fairfax County Industrial Advisory Board of the Fairfax County Public Schools. (Fairfax County is a large county in Northern Virginia, just outside the boundary of the District of Columbia). There, I participated with other business leaders to assist the school system. One of our major accomplishments was the formation of the Thomas Jefferson School for Science and Technology. That school has gone on to be one of the finest schools of its type in the country.

Personally, I had observed the education being provided to my three children in the public schools of Fairfax County. For two of them, the education was acceptable, but the third child struggled and received little help. As a businessman, I had observed the educational proficiency of people we hired, many of whom were unprepared for the work we needed performed.

Finally, I observed the continuing decline of America's competitiveness in the world markets. All these factors led me to take an interest in our public schools.

Since my wife and I wanted to return to Seattle, my involvement in public education became narrowed to "public education in Seattle." This led to the next question, "What are you going to do in public education in Seattle?" I did not know the answer to that question and so set out to do an intense study of the subject.

My first effort was to make a phone call to Lamar Alexander, then Secretary of Education and now the senior senator from Tennessee. At the time, my home was 20 minutes from his office. My phone call yielded a short meeting with the Secretary and an extensive meeting with the Deputy Secretary, David Kearns. David had been the CEO of Xerox Corporation prior to becoming Deputy Secretary. He and I met on three separate occasions in 1992 to discuss public education. He also provided me with several names of people to whom I should speak. This began what became an odyssey into the world of education. Over the next two years, I talked with hundreds of educational leaders, including the heads of the two national teachers unions, I traveled to 19 states, met with five governors, visited over 100 of America's finest schools, both public and private and met with the deans and faculty of two dozen education schools. I also read every book or report people recommended to me.

In my travels, I saw islands of excellence surrounded by a sea of mediocrity. I saw wonderful people doing amazing work, but in spite of the system, not because of it. Generally, when I visited an outstanding school, I found a principal who acknowledged that he or she had to break some rules to achieve the goals they wanted. They would give teachers far more autonomy than was allowed, they would allocate resources differently than specified, often they used different curricula than mandated, etc. Nonetheless, they did it inside the system. Many of these schools would give any private school a run for their money. Such schools, many of which were in destitute neighborhoods with a large proportion of poor and minority children, were fountains of hope for their students. Learning was occurring in every classroom and there was an excitement in both the children and the teachers. But, I also saw a rigid bureaucratic system that resisted change.

As I delved further, I arrived at two conclusions. The first was the notion that to make a different in public education you must get inside the system. I based this assumption on witnessing thousands, if not tens of thousands of people who were doing their level best to help improve their schools, to no avail. I saw this all over the country and concluded that I had to get inside the system.

Quickly, I learned that I was not qualified to be a teacher (I was the president of a New York Stock Exchange Company and had a Harvard MBA, but did not have a teaching certificate), nor was I qualified to be a principal. (I had no principal certification). In 1993, no one would consider me as a candidate for superintendent. So, the only entry point available to someone like me was to run for the school board.

Next, I learned that most of the problems of our schools were in the urban systems where over half of our children go to school and where the vast majority of minorities attend school. So, I concluded I would run for the school board in an urban system. Since my wife and I wanted to live in Seattle, it was going to be the school board of the Seattle Public Schools.

With the decision to run for the school board, it was necessary for me to return to Seattle and establish residence so I could file for public office. However, my residence had to be in the district I was to represent. In Seattle, there are seven school board members and each one represents a district within the city. I decided, that if I was going to win election, I had to run in a district where the incumbent did not seek re-election. This was important since I had been gone from the city for almost 23 years and no one knew my name or anything about me.

As fate would have it, the only incumbent who chose not to run in 1993, was the one who represented the district where both my wife and I had grown up and where we wanted to live again. Thus, we now live about a half-mile from my wife's childhood home.

In 1993, I ran and was elected to the Seattle School Board where I served for eight years. At the time of my election, the school district had approximately 45,000 students, a budget of $297 million, with about 100 schools and 4,600 employees.

When I ran for the board, I had an agenda that I shared with my colleagues. This agenda had been developed from my travels. The first item on that agenda was to hire a new superintendent. The current superintendent was a wonderful man, but he was not a change agent. He had been superintendent for 11 years and the Seattle Public Schools had not materially improved under his leadership. I felt we needed a "change agent" if we were going to make major improvements.

It took a year for a majority of my colleagues to agree with me that we needed new leadership. Once we had the votes, it then became a question of the search. Washington State is one of only five states that does not require a superintendent to be certified. Thus, we were free to look outside education for our new leader. In fact, because I had traveled the country extensively looking for a district that had taken school reform to scale, I was able to absolutely assure my colleagues that the person we were looking for was not in public education. Had he or she been there, I would have found them.

To ensure we would see candidates from outside the field of public education, the board selected a business search firm, as opposed to an education search firm. We told the firm to bring us a non-traditional leader. They found him in the form of retired General John Stanford.

Stanford had been in the Army for 25 years, retiring as a Major General and then became the county executive of Fulton County, Georgia (the county which includes the city of Atlanta). During his tenure as county executive, Stanford had been able to move the county from the bottom third of counties in their financial ratings to the upper 10 percent. He had also funded over $1.0 billion of infrastructures for the county without raising taxes. In other words, here was a proven leader who had turned around a public system. Exactly the type of person we wanted.

John was hired and became superintendent in September of 1995. Though he only served two-and-a-half years (he died quickly after being diagnosed with acute leukemia), he helped orchestrate numerous changes that were implemented during his tenure and the three years following his death.

In addition to hiring a new superintendent, below is a partial list of what else we accomplished:

1. **Eliminated mandatory busing.** This was our first vote after John became superintendent. What we had learned was that 10 times more minorities were being bused than whites and that the academic achievement of those being bused was not appreciably higher than those not bused.

2. **Decentralized the system.** Too many decisions were being made at the district headquarters. We empowered our principals and gave them both authority and responsibility for how their school performed.

3. **Modified the union contract.** We were able to negotiate a change in the union contract that allowed principals to hire staff without regard to seniority. This was a big win and a necessary win because it was impossible to hold principals accountable if they had no authority over staffing.

4. **Changed how schools were funded.** When I was elected, the funding system used was called a *staffing model*. That meant that the money budgeted to a school was based upon the number of adults assigned to that school. Adult assignment was based upon student population. Twenty-five students equaled one teacher. Five hundred students called for an assistant principal. This funding model made no sense and so we changed it to a *weighted student-funding model*. This model moved the money with the students and it took into account that certain students cost more to educate than do others. What this system yielded was more money for those schools that had the toughest students to teach. Just the reverse of what had been occurring.

5. **Adopted choice.** We recognized that parents, not the district, should be able to decide where their child attends school. This system, which gave a preference to the neighborhood school, allowed parents to send their child to any school they wanted to, provided their was room and provided they could get their child to the building. If a child attended school outside their "catchment" area, there would be no transportation provided. This move put pressure on the schools to create a learning environment that parents wanted their child to have. It meant that schools had to attract parents or they would not be funded. It forced schools to do a self-analysis and create programs that attracted parents and children.

6. **Established a Principal Training Institute.** Because we had dramatically changed the job of being a principal, it was necessary that we provide training to our principals to teach them how to budget and how to interview and hire staff—two tasks they had not been trained for and had never done.

7. **Passed levies.** Seattle Schools normally tried to pass two levies every four years. One was an operating levy that was used to supplement state funding. The other was a capital levy that was used for new construction and major maintenance. Three prior capital levies had failed to pass. Shortly after Stanford's arrival, we put on the ballot a $339 million capital levy that passed. With that money, we were able to build or remodel 17 schools with the entire program coming in on time and on budget.

8. **Installed standards for every grade.**

9. **Reduced the dropout rate.**

10. **Reduced truancy rates.**

11. **Increased enrollment for the first time in 25 years.**

Those were the major changes we made and, because of our progress, the Seattle schools were being recognized nationally as a district on the move.

I retired from the Board in 2001. Upon my retirement, the *Seattle Times* wrote an editorial (November 30, 2001):

> When Seattle School Board President Don Nielsen joined the board, the seasoned businessman made no bones about using this city as a template to transform education nationwide.
>
> He got part of the way.
>
> A look at the changes in the district during Nielsen's eight-year tenure as a leader and provocateur on the board is a reminder why, when he retires next month, his expertise will be missed.
>
> The district has come a long way toward being a quality system, and Nielsen deserves a large part of the credit."

It has now been 13 years since I served on the Seattle School Board. In that time, with the exception of mandatory busing and the modification to the union contract, virtually everything we put in place has been radically modified, terminated or reversed. It's as if we were never there. New board members and new superintendents have come and gone and each has had their own agenda. The net effect is that Seattle's public schools and the system under which they operate are now very much like they were prior to 1993. What's even more painful to recognize is that this situation is not unique to Seattle. It happens in every city that has attempted massive change. Thus, the status quo is the only sustainable outcome.

Seeing all our work go for naught has caused me to change my thoughts on how we need to go about improving our schools. Initially, I thought one had to get inside the system to make a difference. I also thought the urban system was the entity of change. Basically, I have been proven wrong on both assumptions. Getting inside the system is no guarantee you can do anything of a sustainable nature and the urban system is definitely not the primary entity of change.

This has been a painful lesson, but a necessary one for me to really understand where the problems lie and what we need to do to change them. What I have concluded is that the entity of change is the state, not the district, not the school and not the federal government. The state is the primary funder of schools and it is also the entity that controls who can and who cannot work in our schools. It is the state that must change laws to allow schools the freedom to be good, to be innovative, to adjust to the needs of their students, to effectively educate every child in *every school*.

This book is written to give state leaders a template on what laws to change and to show how state leaders can enact laws and regulations to provide sustainable improvement in our public schools.

PART ONE:

THE CURRENT LANDSCAPE

1.

THE EXISTING SYSTEM

Figure 1:
Trends in spending, staffing and enrollment since 1970

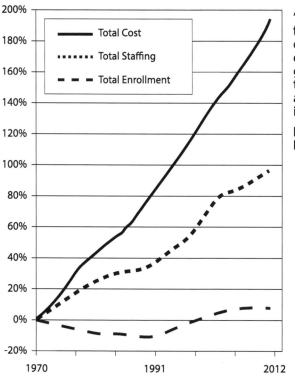

"Total cost" is the full amount spent on K-12 education of a student graduating in the given year, adjusted for inflation.

In 1970: $56,903
In 2010: $165,426

Source: National Center for Education Statistics
Digest of Education Statistics 2012
Table 202 – Total Cost
Table 35 – Total Staffing
Table 35 – Total Enrollment

I<small>N</small> F<small>IGURE</small> 1, <small>WE CAN SEE THAT DURING THE LAST</small> 42 <small>YEARS, THERE</small> has been an enormous increase in the amount of money being invested in the education of our children. However, during that time, there has been no meaningful increase in the number of students in our schools. Thus, we are now spending almost 190% more per child to educate our children than was the case in 1970. We can also see that most of that money has gone to pay for the increased number of adults now working in our public education system. We now have almost twice as many adults per student as we did in 1970. Growth in adult employment has grown four times faster than student enrollment.

In spite of these major increases in both money and staffing, there has been no appreciable improvement in the academic achievement of our children as shown in Figure 2.

Figure 2:
Trends in reading scores since 1970

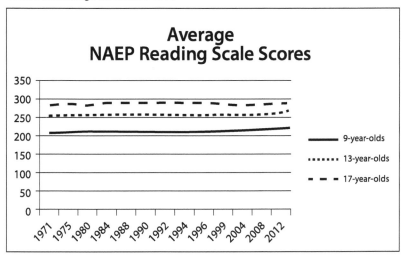

Source: National Center for Education Statistics
Digest of Education Statistics 2012

One is forced, therefore, to conclude that improved academic achievement is not going to happen if we continue to put more money into the system or hire more people to work on the issue. Obviously, the problem with our schools is not about money or staffing.

As a student of our public education system and former school board member, I had the privilege of visiting over a hundred schools in states across the country. Some of these were America's finest schools. Students in those schools were receiving an excellent public education regardless of their race, ethnic origin, or socioeconomic status.

Visiting and observing these schools, I came to realize that public education can work. In our country, we have hundreds of wonderful public schools. In fact, almost every city has at least one, if not several, outstanding schools. Sadly, however, these schools are the exception not the norm. The best of these schools have been thoroughly examined in various books, most of which now occupy space in my home library.

Seeing that the United States has wonderful schools as part of the public system, I sought to find an entire school district that operated as effectively. I wanted to find a district in which all the schools, not just one or two, possessed the characteristics I had observed in high-performing schools.

After devoting nearly a year to the search, I found only one district that had endeavored to create an entire system that operated as effectively as the individual high-performing schools I had visited. That district was in Vance County, North Carolina, located about 60 miles north of Durham. The year was 1993. Then Superintendent Betty Wallace (she was subsequently fired) had transformed a whole education system in three years, and the results were astounding. When Betty assumed leadership of the district, Vance County Schools were rated in the bottom 10 percent of all schools in North Carolina and were at risk of being taken over by the state. Betty came in with a plan, and in three years Vance County Schools had improved so much the district was rated in the middle of all North Carolina school districts.

Vance County is a small rural area. At the time I visited this 7000-student district, about 60 percent of the students served were African American, and about the same percentage of students lived in poverty. The area had two high schools, two middle schools and ten elementary schools. Betty wrote about her experiences in Vance County and described her strategy for transforming public schools. Her book is called *The Poisoned Apple*, and I highly recommend it.

Visiting Vance County Schools and talking at length with Betty Wallace firmly convinced me that it is possible to transform an entire school district for the better. She did it, albeit on a small scale, and in doing so, she created a practical template that others could use.

Betty was fired a couple of years later following her decision to terminate a black school administrator. The administrator had been accused of sexual harassment. Betty's investigation of the charges gave her reason to believe they were valid, and she terminated the individual. Subsequently, the school board (comprised of a majority of black members) decided to side with the administrator and fired Betty for wrongful dismissal.

Betty's ideas are as applicable today as they were when she implemented them back in the early 1990s. She knew the problem of low-performing schools is not that the children can't learn; it is the structure of the system and the constraints imposed on the adults operating within that system. She also knew that unless that system is dramatically modified, the effective education of all children is impossible. Betty worked on turning around a district, and she succeeded. After she left, however, the district soon went back to its old low-performance levels and, once again, began to fail the very children it was set up to serve. I experienced the same phenomenon in Seattle. Others have also seen the same thing occur—temporary success that is subsequently reversed. Sustainable change is virtually impossible within the present system.

Despite these setbacks, we must change the system because it is failing our children and our nation. Here is a review of the extent of the problem:

- Only 26 percent of high school graduates meet the college readiness benchmarks in all four subjects of the ACT Test (English, reading, mathematics and science).[12]

- Only 27 percent of fourth-graders and 32 percent of eighth-graders are proficient in reading, and fully 32 percent of fourth-graders and 22 percent of eighth-graders score "below basic."[13]

- Over 3.0 million students drop out of high school annually.[14]

- The U.S. now ranks 24th out of all developed nations in the education proficiency of our students—just ahead of Lithuania.[15]

- The U.S. spends 39 percent more per pupil than Germany, 33 percent more than France, and 39 percent more than Japan.[16]

- The United States has the largest per-capita prison population in the world, followed by Russia. The highest-scoring European countries in international education comparisons tend to be those with the lowest prison populations.[17]

Let's take a look at this system that is so badly in need of transformation.

Today's school system operates very much like a production line in an early twentieth-century factory. Every student, regardless of ability or preparation, attends school for the same length of time each day, each week and each year. Every student is taught to the same curriculum, delivered in much the same way, and we expect the same outcome for nearly every child.

---

12. "Condition of College & Career Readiness 2013," http://www.act.org/research/policymakers/cccr13/readiness1.html.
13. National Assessment of Educational Progress, *The Nation's Report Card, 2013* Mathematics and Reading, 7.
14. *Education Week*, Children Trends Database, January, 2014. http://www.statisticbrain.com/high-school-dropout-statistics/.
15. PTSA 2012 Results In Focus: What 15-Year-Olds Know and What They Can Do With What They Know, OECD 2014, 5.
16. Organization for Economic Cooperation and Development. *OECD Factbook Statistics,* (2013), http://www.oecd-ilibrary.org.
17. Tom Carroll, "Education Beats Incarceration," *Education Week* (March 26, 2008), 32.

However, any person knowledgeable about production knows the only way a production line works well is if the incoming raw material is uniform in all respects. In education, we have anything but uniform raw material. Our students come from all backgrounds. They have different interests, different learning styles, different motivations, different levels of learning readiness, different home environments, and different amounts of sleep the night before, etc. No two students are really alike, yet our present system treats them virtually the same. **Our present system has never effectively educated every child, and it never will.** In fact, the system was specifically designed not to effectively educate every child, and it has achieved that goal for 130 years.

In repeated efforts to remedy this situation, Congress, state legislatures and local school boards have all put in place thousands of regulations. Each of these regulations was designed to correct a perceived deficiency in the system. These regulations have been piled one upon the other to the extent the system is now tightly handcuffed. Even the best principals and superintendents find it virtually impossible to operate an effective school or district under the current burden of rules, procedures and paperwork.

In fact, all of the effective schools in this country are excellent in spite of the larger system, not because of it. The leaders of these schools regularly break the rules in order to educate their children. Frankly, it is the only way excellence can be achieved.

To substantiate the above points, let's look at the core structure of the current system.

Teaching

To BECOME a teacher in any state, one needs to graduate from an approved college of education and gain *certification*. In most states, this is the only way to become an approved public school teacher. There are a few states with *alternative certification laws*, but these are narrow exceptions and only a small percentage of teachers gain entry into the education system through these alternative means.

The major exception is Teach For America (TFA). This organization hires young people who are some of the top graduates of their respective universities and provides an alternative certification process via training over a summer and then ongoing training during the first year of teaching. Teach for America currently has 11,000 cohorts actively teaching in 25 cities throughout the country. In addition, there has been some recent collaboration with other alternative certification programs and universities. One example is a collaboration occurring at the University of Washington, which is running a revision of the TFA's summer training program and offering it to candidates seeking alternative certification. This instance, however, is one of a limited number of efforts that impact a very small number of potential teachers.

In most states, there are numerous institutions licensed to grant teaching certificates. In Virginia there are 50, and in my state, Washington, we have 22. Pennsylvania has over 90. As a nation, we have over 1400 such schools. The spectrum of quality between the best and the worst teaching institutions in each state is substantial. Moreover, there is no established standard to measure the effectiveness of any given educational training program. Again, there have been some recent moves to change this situation. Both North Carolina and Tennessee have moved to a *value-added measurement* of their education schools. That effort is gaining traction in other states as well.

Teachers gain their certification from their university upon graduation. Certification is a state-mandated requirement and must be met before a graduate can be hired by a school district. Gaining certification, however, simply means one has completed the necessary course of study dictated by the state. It does not mean that a person can actually teach children. **In fact, certified is no guarantee of being qualified.** There are many certified teachers in the profession who are detrimental to the education of children. Again, this is not an all-inclusive statement, as there are many wonderful teachers in the profession. However, most post-secondary education schools do not have any assessment of teaching ability built into their program. Recently, a few states have recognized this issue and have installed what is called the *Teacher Performance Assessment* (TPA) or similar names. This is a relatively new effort and is being met by resistance from many education schools.

To graduate from a typical education school, the student must spend time teaching in a real classroom. It is called *student teaching*. These programs vary in length, but six weeks is not uncommon. A student may student teach in a second-grade class, but upon graduation, that same student may be hired to teach a fourth-grade class. This experience disconnect often happens and the effect is to put a new teacher into a classroom to work with students of an age she has never taught before, with a curriculum she has never seen before, in a school she has never visited.

Moreover, when a new teacher comes into a school, her students' previous teacher seldom provides any information about the class. To make matters worse, most districts do not supply the new teacher with meaningful lesson plans or details on how to teach the curriculum. That same new teacher will likely not be given a mentor, and more than likely be assigned to the toughest classes in the lowest-performing schools. This is a recipe for failure.

In fact, thirty percent of teachers leave the profession within five years. In urban school systems, fifty percent leave within five years.[18] It is not hard to understand why.

Finally, data also tells us the graduates who performed best in college of education programs are the first students to leave the profession.[19]

Though there are many gifted teachers in our classrooms today, there are not nearly enough. As long as the most gifted education stu-

18. National Commission on Teaching and America's Future, "No Dream Denied: A Pledge to America's Children, Summary Report," (Washington, DC: NCTAF, 2003), 10.
19. Ibid., 13.

dents leave the teaching profession early and as long as our brightest and most talented citizens are not entering the profession of teaching at all, we will not dramatically improve the quality of classroom instruction in our public schools.

Leadership

EVERY ORGANIZATION needs leadership. In the school system that leadership is provided by principals and superintendents.

Principal

To become a principal also requires certification from an approved school of education. However, to gain admission for principal training, one must first have been a teacher for at least three years. In other words, one must have attended an education school, become certified, and survived the first three years of teaching.

Principal certification is usually a one-year program and graduates receive either a master's degree in School Administration or simply a principal certificate. Again, the only place you can get such a certificate is at an education school. As was the case with teachers, the spectrum of quality between the best and worst principal training programs is substantial.

At most schools of education, there are no other qualifications needed to become a principal. One does not need to present recommendations from a principal or superintendent, nor have demonstrated leadership skills, nor have been an outstanding teacher. One merely needs to have taught for three years and have enough money to pay the tuition. Because many schools of education need students' tuition, to apply is to be accepted, to be accepted is to graduate, and to graduate, because of the demand for principals, is to get hired. In most states a principal receives tenure in just three years, meaning public school students and teachers will have that person in a leadership position for 20 to 30 years.

As a consequence of this system, what we have in education is **leadership by accident not by design**. It is the only system in our society that I know of where **promotion is done by self-selection**. Nearly every teacher who seeks to become a tenured principal will become one, regardless of their lack of leadership and management skills. One exception to this statement is the Education School of the University of Washington, which has the Danforth Program for school leadership.[20] This program has some selectivity in admission requirements and is now issuing a "money-back guarantee" that their graduates will be effective principals. This is a brand new effort by the Danforth program and it is too soon to determine its validity.

Superintendent

In most states, the principal self-selection process repeats itself at this level. Forty five of the fifty states require that superintendents must be certified and this is again obtained by attending an approved school of education. Most superintendent candidates receive a PhD or an EdD in Education, many with a major in curriculum studies. One can self-select into most of these programs just as easily as signing up for principal training.

Few schools of education have any meaningful leadership training programs and few recognize how different the job of superintendent is from other management positions, particularly in urban school systems. Superintendent candidates should receive training in organizational behavior, labor relations, finance and budgeting, technology, construction contracting, etc. Few, if any, of these kinds of skills are taught in schools of education. Once again, public school districts end up with leadership by accident not by design.

Schools of education hold a monopoly on both the supply of teachers and of leaders for our schools. As will be detailed later, this single source of supply poses a major impediment to improving our schools.

We will talk more about education leadership in Chapter 6.

---

20. http://www.danforth.uw.edu

Governance

SCHOOL DISTRICTS are governed by school boards. School board members are elected by the citizens of the community and generally serve four-year terms. School boards are set up to be policy-making bodies, but they regularly delve into operations. Candidates for school board are often ill-equipped to serve in a leadership capacity, resulting in a district's governance needs being unmet.

The membership of school boards often changes as election cycles occur. Quite often, a majority of a board is changed in one election. When that happens, the policy direction of the district often changes. Sometimes, a board's new majority decides to hire a new superintendent. This regularly occurs in urban systems where the average tenure of a superintendent is only 3.6 years.[21] This high turnover of school board membership and of superintendents makes long-term improvement in the quality of public education very difficult, if not impossible.

Centralization

SCHOOL DISTRICTS in this country are set up as centralized bureaucratic institutions. Virtually all decisions are made at the central office. Principals seldom have much authority over people, money or curriculum, but they are expected to be accountable for how their school performs. Any management professional would recognize immediately that this arrangement is simply not reasonable. To effectively lead and manage any organization, the leader should have authority over hiring and a major portion of the budget. Few principals are granted such autonomy. Realistically, in most districts, principals only control the opening of the school each day and ensuring that the school operates smoothly.

Supposedly, principals act as education leaders of their school. Some perform this function very well, but many do not. It is ludicrous to hold a principal accountable for the performance of the school's teaching staff when the top manager is awarded no control over personnel, no control over the curriculum, and little-to-no control over money. Decisions in

---

21. "Council of Great City Schools," *Urban Indicator* (Fall 2010), 2.

all of these areas are generally made at the central district level. This top-down situation, combined with the myriad of regulations imposed upon schools by both state and federal organizations, creates a system that perpetuates mediocrity and discourages innovation.

Joseph Olchefske, former superintendent of the Seattle Public Schools, describes America's education system as a "Soviet Union model" system. The former Soviet Union ran a national economy based upon a centralized system. In that system, large numbers of people were employed, but little work got done and those tasks that were performed were not done well.

This analogy, to a school district, has considerable validity. A classic example of what I am talking about is occurring in New York. There, the city school system has more administrators than the entire nation of France and the state has more administrators than all the nations in Western Europe combined.[22] Moreover, the New York City Public School System, with 1,000,000 students, has a central office staff of 6,000. The Archdiocese of New York, with 200,000 students, has 35.[23]

Time

SCHOOLS ARE run on a time-based system as opposed to a learning-based system.

The School Day:

In almost all schools, the school day is six hours. The starting and stopping times vary between districts and between elementary and secondary schools, but the net amount of time, regardless of when the day starts, is six hours. In secondary school, the day is divided into periods of one hour (actually 50–55 minutes). In most schools, a period ends with the ringing of a bell, and then the students move to another class to attend another period. One period will cover one subject. Students may take

---

22. David Kirkpatrick, "The Superintendency: Neither Inevitable Nor Necessary," U.S. Freedom Foundation (September 30, 2004), 1, http://www.freerepublic.com/focus/f-news/1325624/posts.
23. Ibid., 1.

English in first period, math in second period, history in third period, etc. In elementary school, the rigidity of this schedule is reduced as students normally have only one teacher and attend class in only one classroom. This situation tends to give elementary teachers more flexibility in terms of the time spent on a given subject in any given day. However, in secondary school, the day is generally fixed to a proscribed schedule of six periods. This situation forces teachers to develop lesson plans that will only take one period to deliver. The driver here is time, not learning. Teachers are forced to use the period to convey the lesson of the day. Some students may learn the lesson in 10 minutes; others may not understand it after 50 minutes. It doesn't matter. The period ends and the students have to leave to go to their next class.

Learning takes a back seat to time. The clock drives what occurs and, as a consequence, students soon learn that their learning and understanding is secondary to the teacher's need to cover the material. The lesson being controlled by time impacts a student's ability to achieve. If a student is a fast learner in English, but a slow learner in math, the present system will fail the student's learning in both subjects. A slow learner in math will quickly get turned off to the subject because they can't keep up. Ultimately, they will come out of high school under-educated in a core subject. Conversely, a fast learner in math may be equally turned off because they get bored waiting for the class to progress.

The School Year:

The school year is 178–180 days, just slightly less than half a calendar year. The school year, was originally set to comply with the student's need to help parents with farm labor and other tasks needed for the family to survive. In the early days of the twentieth century, this made sense. Young people didn't need a lot of education to survive, and there was always plenty of work to do at home. Today, however, that is no longer the case. Only three percent of America's families now work on the farm. Moreover, the educational needs of young people, including those who will become farmers, have grown exponentially during the twentieth century, but we still have the same school year. This school year means that our children are out of school 81 days a year or about 16 school weeks: 365 − 104 (for weekends) − 180 = 81.

Other industrialized nations have determined that a 180-day school year is insufficient. The education year for young people in other countries is quite different from what we provide to our children. From the longest to the shortest, the school year for other major nations is as follows:

Korea—220

Japan—200

Germany—193

England—190

Finland—189

Canada—183

USA—180[24]

The United States has the shortest school year in the developed world. Moreover, in many cases the school day is also longer in other countries. In Japan, for example, students go to school more hours per day, more days per week, and more weeks per year than do American students. The net effect is that a Japanese child, upon graduation from high school, will have attended school for at least two American school years more than an American student in the same twelve-year period. It is little wonder that students in other countries are out-performing American students in international exams. The one exception to this statement is the country of Finland where students go to school about the same amount of time as American students yet perform far better on international exams. Finland has extensive preschool programs and

---

24. National Center for Education Statistics, *Digest of Education Statistics 2013*, Table 601.60. For the United States, the actual average for all states is 178, even though most states show 180 days as their school year.

only the brightest of its citizens are allowed to enter into the teaching profession.

The secondary school year is divided into semesters, which is one-half of the year or 90 days. Again, in secondary school, some courses last one semester. It does not matter whether a child can master the subject material in 30 days or instead needs 200 days. All students spend the same time on the course for one semester.

Grades:

The class in which students are placed is also based upon time—only in this case it is really age. If a child is eight years old, that child is placed in the third grade. Not because that is their level of learning readiness, but rather because the child is eight. The child could be reading at the fifth-grade level, doing math at the fourth-grade level, and science at the second-grade level. However, because the child is eight, that child will take all subjects at the third-grade level regardless of how quickly or slowly they learn the material. All grades in our K–12 system are based upon age, not learning readiness or achievement levels.

Graduation:

Graduation from school is also based on time. To graduate, a student needs to collect a certain number of credits (called *Carnegie Units*). A credit is generally based on one year of class time or 9900 minutes of instruction (55 minutes x 180 days). A credit is not a measure of learning; it is a measure of time spent in class. Some refer to it as a "seat time" measure. In other words, to graduate from high school requires that a student spend a specific quantity of seat time in school.

Graduation occurs at the end of the twelfth grade, assuming the student has a sufficient number of credits. Most states require 20 or 21 credits for graduation. Normally, a student needs to earn eight credits in English, six in math, four in science, etc. In fact, students not only need to acquire a certain number of credits to graduate, they need them in the proper subjects. I witnessed a situation in which a student did not graduate because he lacked a half credit in physical education (PE).

What all of this says is that seat time, rather than real learning, is the primary measurement used for meeting graduation requirements. Expressed another way, in public education, measuring input is more important than measuring output.

Group versus Individual

I HAVE described our system of education as a *factory model*. Every child in a class is taught to the same curriculum, delivered the same way for the same length of time each day. However, every child is different. Students arrive at school with widely differing levels of learning readiness. Some pick up reading quickly, others find it very difficult, some find math interesting, others do not, etc. In our system, the student's particular interests and aptitudes are really irrelevant. The group receives the education and if some students understand the material and some do not, that is considered okay. I classify this as the system having a focus on teaching rather than on learning. Again, not every school works this way and certainly not every classroom, but as a total system, this description is accurate.

School Funding

NOT ONLY do principals seldom have control over the money spent within the school building but also, most states fund their public schools in a one-size-fits-all manner. Funding that states provide to districts is generally based on the number of students enrolled in the school system. Some states provide a slight increase in funding for a non-English speaking child and the federal government provides additional money for special education children. None of these funding decisions come anywhere close to recognizing the true differing costs of educating these children.

For example, a child who speaks no English and is entering kindergarten has a relatively easy problem to overcome. However, a student entering high school who does not speak English is another story altogether. In most state-funding patterns, those two children would be funded for the same amount. The same is true for special education children, although there are four levels of funding for these children. A child who has slight dyslexia is one issue, a child who is a paraplegic or a child who is deaf or developmentally disabled is entirely different. Though funding patterns differentiate severely handicapped children from those who are modestly handicapped, the amount of money allocated for the former is nowhere near sufficient for the educational costs incurred. The law requires that these children receive an education, as well they should, but the amount of money provided is insufficient to comply with the law. The net effect is that money is diverted from regular students to help fund the needs of special education students.

States also set compensation and benefit levels for teachers. Salaries for teachers tend to be based upon years of service and credits or advanced degrees attained. Virtually no compensation is tied to real classroom performance, or to the ability of a teacher to advance the learning of children under his or her care.

Conclusion

FROM THE above description, it is easy to understand why so many of our children do not receive the public education they need and deserve. The system is the problem, and unless and until we change it, we will constantly be disappointed by our inability to improve the level of student achievement.

Over the past fifty years, policy makers have initiated dozens of education reform programs, which, once implemented, were supposed to improve student achievement. Many had some positive effect, although some were detrimental. Most did little more than tweak the system, rather than change it. Really good ideas employed in a flawed system will rarely have any meaningful impact. That certainly has been the case with public education. All of the reform ideas of the past four decades have had little, if any, positive impact on student achievement. Also, investing more money into a failed system will simply produce a more expensive failed system.

To summarize five core aspects of public education, what we have is:

1. An adult-focused system, but we need a student-focused system.

2. A time-based system, but we need an achievement-based system.

3. A teaching-focused system, but we need a learning-focused system.

4. A group-based system, but we need an individual-based system.

5. An input-focused system, but we need an output-focused system.

In other words, our present system is wrong and no matter how much we tweak or reform it, it will never meet the needs of our children or of society. To make real progress we must fundamentally transform the public education system.

Changing the system to operate differently in the above five areas will, over time, result in positive changes in all internal and external systems that impact school operations.

It is my belief that the most important institution in our free democratic society is our public school system. Fixing our schools, so they work for all students, is not only the right thing to do for our children, it is the right thing to do for our country.

If we are serious about educating all our children, we must first fundamentally change the existing system of public education.

2.

EXTERNAL FACTORS

OUR PRESENT SYSTEM OF PUBLIC EDUCATION IS OBSOLETE. THAT IS true not only because the school system was designed as a production line and it was designed to meet the needs of an earlier historical era, but also because it was designed for an earlier social era. The historical setting was important, but sweeping societal changes over the past eighty to ninety years have also played a major role in making today's education system even more obsolete, however, they are seldom mentioned in the current debate about how best to improve education. These societal changes greatly influenced our schools, though school administrators had little or no control over them. Thus, they are *external factors*.

In this chapter we will briefly review the major external factors that have had a material impact on our schools' ability to educate our children. The factors below are listed not in order of importance, but rather chronologically. The societal changes require us to rethink how we go about educating our children.

World War II

IN THE decades prior to World War II, our public school system operated pretty well. The school system, as it developed in the late 1800s, provided our country with the educated workers it needed. For almost sixty years, the system worked as designed and the country prospered. Manual labor was the predominat type of work, and the level of learning provided was sufficient.

WWII created an increased need for factory workers, engineers and other technically trained individuals. At the same time, women entered the workforce in unprecedented numbers.

The GI Bill, enacted after the war, created the opportunity for millions of young men and women, often the first in their families, to go to college. The result was an enormous increase in the number of our citizens who had advanced education, and this, in turn, created a significant increase in our productive economy and in our exports of goods and services. Incomes rose, not only because of the increased quality of our workforce, but because many women were now making very good wages and salaries, thereby raising the income and standard of living for their families.

The middle class grew dramatically during this period. Housing became a boom industry as cities expanded and suburbs began to be formed. Also, the size of houses increased dramatically. Cars became affordable for most households and we saw the beginning of the two-car garage and the two-car family. Day care was another growing industry, and many children now spent much of the day with non-family members.

With prosperity came an increasing number of divorces. As the economy came out of the Depression, the unemployment rate declined and the divorce rates increased. In the early part of the twentieth century, divorce affected less than 10 percent of marriages.[25] During the Depression, the rate approached 20 percent. By the end of the War, it had increased to 27 percent and by the mid-1980s, half of all marriages ended in divorce.[26] The impact of a marriage breakup on children is substantial. Increasing numbers of children came to school from single-parent homes. These single parents had less time to spend with their children and even less time to spend at their children's school. Parental involve-

25. U.S. Department of Health and Human Services, National Center for Health Statistics, "Marriages and Divorces, 1900–2009."

26. U.S. Census Bureau, Statistical Abstract of the United States, 2011, Section 2, "Births, Deaths, Marriages and Divorces."

ment in children's education declined. The net effect was more pressure on schools to provide much of the non-academic development and work in raising a child that had formerly been provided in the home.

Women in the Work Force

BEFORE WORLD War II, women were employed outside the home primarily as teachers, nurses and secretaries. Thus, our schools were staffed with many of our most talented women, who became wonderful teachers of our children.

As opportunities for women expanded and more women entered other professions, the number and quality of women entering the teaching profession declined. Though many talented women continued to become teachers, many of the best and brightest were able to find employment in other fields. While this occurred, the post-war baby boom caused a rapid expansion in the number of schools and classrooms throughout the country. The result was more children in class but fewer top-quality teachers to educate them.

The Interstate Highway System

IN 1956, President Eisenhower and Congress passed the Federal Aid Highway Act. This legislation called for the creation of an interstate highway system that began the process of building four-lane, all-weather, divided highways across the country and through virtually every major city.

These new high-speed road systems served to expand the metropolitan area of all our major cities. Middle-class families continued their migration out of our cities to the suburbs, where they could get a bigger house and yard for less money and still be a reasonably short (time-wise) drive from work. The mass exodus from our cities served to decrease the size of urban school systems and served to reduce the number of middle-class children who attended those schools. The families who remained tended to be those who could not afford to move—that is, families living in poverty or newly arrived immigrants.

Urban school districts experienced a decline in revenue (as their tax bases diminished), a decline in attendance by middle-class students, an increase in the percentage of students of color, an increase in students whose primary language was not English and an increase in the number of students being raised in poverty or in very poor economic conditions. These students, for the most part, were coming into school with far less preparation for learning than students whose parents had moved the family to the suburbs. Though the remaining students were perfectly capable of learning, they were less prepared for academic work. Poorly prepared students take more time and effort to educate on the part of teachers, and thus the cost of educating each student was higher than for those who had left the urban school system. This increase in the cost to educate each student combined with the tax-base reduction resulted in a dramatic decline in the quality of education available to students in urban centers.

The Civil Rights Act and Mandatory Busing

WITH PASSAGE of the Civil Rights Act in 1964, school districts that were operating racially segregated schools were required to integrate their schools. The courts and school administrators chose mandatory busing as the policy for accomplishing this. There is no question that ending school segregation and other forms of racial discrimination was the right thing to do. Desegregation was long overdue. However, the way our country implemented the new law often had a profoundly negative impact on the quality of our public schools and on the students the Civil Rights Act was designed to help.

Prior to the implementation of the Act, most African-Americans (particularly in the South) attended segregated schools. These schools were publicly funded, but were not funded to the same level of white schools. Thus, African-American children attended schools where the buildings were not as new or nice as white schools and where the resources available to the children were substantially less. The conditions of schools in Virginia were indicative of schools in many southern states.

Very few black Virginians received any education at all until public schools were established during Reconstruction. Public schools in Virginia were segregated from the outset, apparently without much thought or debate, on the widely-held assumption that such an arrangement would reduce conflict. Of course, public schools were segregated in many other states, both North and South.

Black schools therefore received far less financial support than did white schools. Black schools had fewer books, worse buildings, and less well paid teachers. Ramshackle, segregated schools marked black Virginians with a stigma of inferiority and the status of second-class citizenship that they would have to endure throughout their lives.[27]

As the Act started to be implemented, African-American children would attend an all-white school where their teacher was also certain to be white. Moreover, that teacher likely had never taught an African-American child.

To make matters worse, the law required that schools be integrated throughout a given city, which meant that both white and black students would be removed from their immediate neighborhood and bused to other schools. Parents who had bought homes, based upon their assessment of the nearby schools, were now reconsidering. Some parents chose to comply with the busing requirements, but many (who could afford to do so) refused and took their children out of the urban public school system and either moved to the suburbs or placed their children in private schools. Either decision had a further negative revenue and cost impact on urban public school systems.

The combination of better highways, being able to buy more house for the same or less money, and the imposition of mandatory busing, had the effect of emptying major cities of middle- and upper-class families and the taxes they provided. The schools were severely impacted. Urban school systems were left with the most difficult-to-educate children (those living in poverty and those whose primary language was not English) and a decreasing tax base to pay for it. The effect was urban decay

27. Virginia Historical Society web site: http://www.vahistorical.org/beginnings.black

and we are still suffering from it. For example, today the city of Chicago has a public school system made up of 86 percent children of color and 87 percent children living in poverty.[28]

Many people believe the middle- and upper-class flight from the cities was due to racism. No doubt racism played a role. However, I believe the bigger reason was the failure of government officials to understand who was responsible for a child's education. Most educated parents, Caucasian or minority, recognize that one of their primary responsibilities is to secure a good education for their children. One of the ways parents do that is by picking the school their children will attend. For many families, this is done by choosing the neighborhood in which to live.

When the courts or the school district officials imposed mandatory busing, they took that school selection decision away from parents. **The lesson here is clear. Governments and school officials need to understand that the responsibility for the education of a child rests with parents, not the school, not the district, not the state or federal government. Politicians should be very careful about making rules or laws that infringe on that responsibility.**

The War on Poverty

ALSO IN 1964, Congress launched the so-called "War on Poverty. At the time, sixteen percent of Americans lived below the government measure of poverty. The country's population was approximately 192 million. Thus, almost 33 million people lived in poverty.[29]

In the years since, our country has spent $15 trillion dollars prosecuting the War on Poverty ($12 trillion in spending by the federal government and a further $3 trillion in spending by the states).[30] Moreover, there are now 126 separate government-funded programs designed to

---

28. Nicholas D. Kristof, "Students Over Unions," *New York Times* (September 12, 2012), A31.

29. *U.S. Census Bureau Current Population Survey, 1960–2010*, Annual Social and Economic Supplements.

30. Michael Turner, "How We Spend Nearly $1 Trillion a Year Fighting Poverty—And Fail," *Cato Institute Policy Analysis*, No 694 (April 11, 2012), 1.

fight poverty.[31] Today the United States has a population of about 313 million people and about seventeen percent of our citizens live below the government-defined level of "poverty."[32] That means we now have 20 million more people living in poverty. Thus, after spending almost $15 trillion dollars on the War on Poverty, we are in a worse poverty condition than we were when the war began nearly forty years ago.

In other words, the War on Poverty has been an unmitigated failure. It failed not because it was not a good cause, but because the programs created under it were waging the wrong war. There is no question that persistent poverty was and is a major problem facing our nation. In the 1960s, the government defined the problem correctly, but did not define the source of the problem correctly. To correct poverty, our country established our welfare system and, over time, failed to end poverty while creating millions of welfare-dependent families.

Poverty is defined as having a lack of money, but the cause of poverty is not a lack of money itself, it is the lack of an ability to earn money. If, instead of spending $15 trillion on "anti-poverty" programs, the same amount of money had been spent on improving the effectiveness of our schools and worker-training programs, we would have substantially reduced the poverty rate in this country.

The failure of the War on Poverty has affected our schools in a material way. Children raised in poverty have been shown to be the least-prepared children any school receives. These children seldom have been exposed to books at home, have often not been read to by their parent or parents, and have lived in an environment where learning was not promoted or stressed. In many cases, the home environment is actually detrimental to the child's education.

Schools with high numbers of children from families living in poverty face greater educational challenges than schools composed mostly

---

31. Ibid.
32. *U.S. Census Bureau Current Population Survey, 1960–2010*, Annual Social and Economic Supplements, Number in Poverty and Poverty Rate 1959–2012, Figure 4.

of middle- and upper-class students. Urban school systems, because of the conditions mentioned earlier, have a disproportionate number of these hard-to-teach students.

The Rise of Teachers Unions

Up until the 1970s, most teachers were not required to join a union as a condition of their employment. In fact, until 1969, the National Education Association (NEA), the nation's largest teachers union, was a professional association operated by school administrators. Until then, decisions regarding how schools would operate were made by administrators and elected school board members.[33]

Between 1960 and 1977, union membership grew from virtually zero to almost 70 percent of all teachers.[34] Today, the NEA has a total membership of 3.2 million and has become the most powerful union and political force in the country. The union is now a major force in dictating how local public schools operate and what management practices are and are not allowed in schools. We will further discuss the influential role of unions in Chapter 4.

The Global Economy

In the late 1970s and early 1980s, America was losing its competitive advantage in the global marketplace. As transportation costs declined, foreign-produced goods were able to enter our markets at prices below domestically produced goods. Japan was becoming a powerhouse economically, and other Asian nations were developing extensive manufacturing capabilities. In addition, the quality of products made overseas was, in many cases, even better than those produced here. The net effect was a massive decline in the quantity of American manufacturing, as more and more foreign goods entered our markets and our own manufacturing companies moved production offshore in order to remain competitive. As companies moved production off-shore, urban centers saw a

---

33. Terry Moe, *Special Interest: Teachers Unions and America's Public Schools* (Washington, DC: Brookings Institution Press, 2011), 48.
34. Ibid., 49

major decline in middle-class jobs. Urban centers were particularly hard-hit by this trend, and their schools again lost the children of middle-class families.

While this trend was occurring, a modern service economy was developing. The vast majority of jobs in this sector were low paying, unskilled positions. People living in poverty or near-poverty, and recently arriving immigrants filled jobs in the service sector. The growth of this sector fueled an increase in immigration, particularly of Hispanic and Southeast Asian families. These new arrivals were largely uneducated or undereducated adults. Upon arrival, their children were enrolled in our public schools, particularly in urban centers. The service sector of the economy continued to grow as we entered the Information Age.

The Information Age

As COMPUTERS came into use and the Information Age was born, we saw an increasing need for our young people to be trained in science and math. Demand for workers with these skills increased dramatically, as did the compensation offered for this type of work. This further exacerbated the gulf between people working in low-paying jobs in the service sector (or living on welfare) and skilled workers making increasing amounts of money in the information sector. As jobs in this high-tech industry grew and became increasingly important, the gap between the haves and have-nots expanded again.

In our schools, money was being spent on technology and science. However, it was largely in the suburbs, as most urban systems were housed in old buildings with antiquated electrical systems and little money available to rewire buildings and/or acquire technology. Students attending urban schools fell further and further behind. Even in urban schools where new technology was put in place, many of the teachers were ill equipped to utilize it effectively. We'll discuss this issue further in Chapter 10.

Immigration Policies

BEFORE WWII, people could immigrate to the United States provided the paperwork was complete, certain requirements were met, and the immigrant quota the U.S. had set for their home country was not filled.

That policy affected my own family. In 1927, my father, who was born in Denmark, wanted to come to the United States to learn English. He found he could not enter the U.S. that year because the quota for Danes was filled. The next country he chose, Canada, had similar policies to those in the U.S., and, although the quota for Danes had not yet been reached, Canada would not let him enter without a sponsor and a job. He was able to secure both and immigrated to Manitoba where he worked on a farm, owned by a Danish immigrant. After WWII my family immigrated to the U.S.

The story of my father is not unique to that era. Immigration laws were stringent and entry quotas were set for nearly every country. Over the last fifty years, immigration quota policy has changed dramatically.

Beginning with the Korean War and continuing since, this country has opened its borders. Millions of immigrants have come to the U.S. by simply walking in, by being picked up in boats and by receiving transportation assistance from family members already here. These new immigrants came mostly from Latin America and Asia. Countries such as Vietnam, Cambodia, Korea, the Philippines, the Pacific Islands, Mexico, Honduras and Brazil, were all sources of new immigrants to this country.

In almost every case, these immigrants were the poor of their countries and few had been provided any meaningful level of education. Most could not read or write in their native language, let alone in English.

These immigrants arrived and began to fill jobs in the service economy. By finding positions as maids, janitors, gardeners, farm workers, etc., these hard-working adults could earn a living without learning to speak English. Though most of these immigrants found jobs, they did not earn incomes that lifted them out of poverty. As a consequence, the children of these new families entered our schools not speaking English well and not well prepared to learn. In states such as Florida, Texas, Arizona and California, Hispanic children are now the dominant population in some public schools, and they make up more than half of the students in some school districts.

We now have schools in major cities where the student population is 100 percent minority children and where 80–90 percent of those children qualify for free or reduced lunches (one of the federal government's measures of poverty). Schools face a very difficult challenge in educating these children. Not only are the children likely to be behind in their learning, they may also not speak English. When I was on the school board in Seattle, we had over 70 different languages spoken by children in our schools.

African-American Population Growth

WHILE THESE momentous events were taking place, the U.S. African-American population continued to grow. Today, America is home to 40 million African Americans. These citizens have suffered from racism and discrimination for centuries, and, though equality is now the law of the land, racism's tragic legacy still affects our society and our schools.

Prior to 1867, few blacks had an opportunity to receive a good education and in some states it was illegal to teach a slave to read. For the next 80 years, most black children were educated in segregated schools. (Some black schools were excellent, but most were underfunded and under-resourced.) With the passage of the Civil Rights Act, African-Americans gained access to integrated schools, but in most cases they still did not receive the same education as white students. Many teachers tended to treat them differently by having lower expectations, and the overall system did not understand the African-American culture.

A large percentage of African Americans were born out of wedlock and were raised by a single parent. That trend has continued and today,

72.2 percent of African American children are born out of wedlock.[35] Many black children are raised by a single parent. Often that single parent is also employed outside the home, which further reduces the time spent with the children. This situation further inhibits the learning readiness of these children, which increases their educational needs when they arrive at school.

Like the Hispanics and Asians mentioned above, African-American families predominately live in urban settings. We are now nearing the end of the third generation of African Americans who have had full access to a public school education. Though progress had been made, there still exists a major gap between the educational attainment of African-Americans and both whites and Asians.

Hispanics are now the largest minority group, surpassing African Americans, and they have a similar social profile both in terms of out-of-wedlock birth rate (53 percent),[36] and the number of children raised in poverty. Hispanic families often struggle with the added problem of not speaking English.

Individuals with Disabilities Education Act (IDEA)

OVER THE years, Congress has enacted numerous laws that have impacted schools. In fact, for most public school systems, the federal government accounts for about 50 percent of the regulations governing the operation of schools, yet it provides less than 10 percent of the funding. At one time, I suggested to my colleagues on the Seattle School Board that we consider not accepting any federal money so we could rid ourselves of all these regulations. My colleagues did not agree with that idea, but I was, and still am, convinced that federal regulations cost local school districts an amount much more than they receive in funding.

---

35. Roger Clegg, "Latest Statistics on Out of Wedlock Births," The Corner, *National Review Online* (October 11, 2013).
36. Caroline May, "Number of Children Born Out of Wedlock In The U.S. Is Soaring," *Business Insider* (February 12, 2012), 1.

Of all the acts passed by Congress, the most onerous for schools is the Individuals with Disabilities Education Act (IDEA). This law requires public schools to provide an education to children with disabilities. One cannot argue with the goal of the law. The problem is with the lack of funding provided and the regulations covering these children.

Children with disabilities deserve the best education we can provide, just as all children do. However, we need to recognize that children with disabilities present new and difficult problems both to the classroom teacher and to the school and school district.

Children who are blind, deaf, or disabled physically and mentally add another dimension to the task of educating all children. In some cases, a child with disabilities will require a one-on-one, full-time teacher. Such children typically cost a school district between $50,000 and $80,000 a year, yet most districts are given only a fraction of that for the child. Even so, the district is required by law to provide for the child's education. As a result, school districts must allocate money from regular students to fund the educational needs of their students with disabilities. Also, the law does not take into account the difference in cost between educating a mentally disabled child and of educating a physically disabled child. The latter may add some expense in a classroom, but the former can be debilitating to the learning of all students in any classroom.

Handicapped students, particularly those with mental disabilities, require instruction from a very specialized and gifted teacher. Teachers like these are in short supply, so teachers who have received little or no training in special education often end up trying to teach these children. This situation is unfair to the teachers, to the child and the child's parents, and to the other children in the classroom.

The need to educate disabled children tends to occur mostly in urban school systems, where administrators are least able to cover the extra costs involved. Urban school systems face this dilemma because most hospitals are located in large cities. Parents with disabled children often position their family's home near these medical centers and enroll their children in the local school system.

Technology

PERHAPS NO change in our society has affected learning more than the advent of advanced technology. Today, young people have the world at their fingertips and they potentially can be learning 24/7. Most of us who are middle-aged or above find we need a younger person's help when we have a technical problem with our computer, cell phone or DVR. Today's young people are growing up in a technological world, but our schools have not kept pace. Technology, in my opinion, is the greatest improvement in individualizing education since that which occured in the older, one-room schoolhouse. Neither the infrastructure of our schools nor the competency of our teaching corps is keeping pace with this new phenomenon. Technology has the potential to revolutionize learning and redefine the meaning of school—in fact, has already done so. We'll discuss this issue more in Chapter 10.

Culture

THOUGH WE seldom talk about it, culture plays a big role in the academic achievement of children and is something over which schools have no control. For example, we see that Asian children routinely perform at high academic levels while African-American and Hispanic children often perform at low levels. Much of this difference occurs within the culture of these different student populations. Asians, particularly ethnic Chinese, Japanese and Koreans, have a culture based on close family ties, and where education is stressed from the moment a child is born. Adult family members work hard to ensure the successful education of their children. This seems to occur regardless of the education level attained by the adult members of the family.

This focus on education manifests itself in the performance of Asian children who consistently outperform other demographics, particularly Hispanics and African-Americans. Part of this difference can be attributed to the high level of poverty and single-parent households, but one must also acknowledge that culture plays a big role in the different outcomes.

The impact of family culture is immediate and begins at birth. Children raised in a typical high-poverty home (often a single-parent minority household) are exposed to less than one-third the number of words that would usually occur in a home where both parents are white and have earned a college degree. Similarly, children in these two types of homes are exposed to totally different learning experiences, with the latter having a much broader knowledge base on which to draw by the time they enter kindergarten.

Also, throughout our society, the increase in the number of families with both parents working is having an impact on our culture. In 1996, a study done by Laurence Steinberg of Temple University showed that one in three parents are totally disengaged from the life of their adolescent child, especially the child's education.[37] Though the data from 1996 is not recent, there is no new evidence to suggest this cultural situation has improved.

"Widespread parental disengagement has left a large proportion of adolescents far more susceptible to the influence of their friends than in past generations, and this influence is taking its toll on school achievement."[38] As Steinberg says, "No curriculum overhaul, no instructional innovation, no change in school organization, no toughening of standards, no rethinking of teacher training or compensation will succeed if students do not come to school interested in, and committed to, learning."[39]

As the population of the country has become more diverse, the impact of culture plays an increasingly important role in the ability of public schools to educate all of our children. In the near term, public schools

---

37. Laurence Steinberg, "Student Beliefs/Character Education," Hoover Institution, 118, http://media.hoover.org/sites/default/files/documents/0817928723_117.pdf.
38. Ibid., 118.
39. Ibid., 120.

will have little, if any, opportunity to influence the culture significantly. Over time however, if our schools effectively educate every child, the cultural differences among races and ethnic groups will diminish as a more unified American culture is reestablished.

Conclusion

ALL THESE external factors have materially impacted our public schools, particularly schools located in urban centers.

Today we are pressing for better performance from our schools. We are installing new standards for learning and demanding more accountability from our educators. Given these trends we need to recognize that, at the very time when we want and need the most highly educated workforce in our history, we are dealing with the most difficult to educate population of children this country has ever seen.

We naturally tend to compare today's schools with those of yesteryear, but that approach is flawed. Today we have many more regulations than in the past. Unions are strong at all levels of the education system and have negotiated strong constraints on management. We have far more children who don't speak English as a first language. We have many more children being raised in poverty and/or in single-parent families. We have more children living in homes where education is not stressed. And we have more special needs children to educate, a task for which our schools were not designed and for which most of our educational staff has not been trained. Finally, we are asking our schools to provide many services to students that formerly were provided at home. All this is occurring when our society and our economy need to have children learn at higher levels than ever before. Taken together, this presents us with a daunting challenge.

In spite of all these trends, I believe the public education system can be made to work, because I have seen it work in individual schools and it is working in several other countries. In the rest of this book, I will lay out the policy changes I believe are necessary to make the system work for all children. I will also suggest that unless and until the system is changed, we should not put large amounts of new money into the existing outdated system. Increasing the funding for a flawed system simply makes running our schools more expensive, without yielding any real improvement for children.

3.

THE MISSION OF SCHOOL

THE MISSION OF SCHOOL MAY SEEM SIMPLE. HOWEVER, I FOUND very little agreement on what is the mission of school. In fact, I would argue that this lack of a common understanding is one of the major reasons schools and school districts fail to effectively educate such a large percentage of their students. The development and solid support of a mission statement is, in my opinion, essential to improving the educational attainment of students served by our public schools.

As I traveled around the country, I asked hundreds of people involved in education the simple question, "What is the mission of school?" I asked because I was genuinely interested in knowing what we were trying to do with school. I had never thought about that question before, but I assumed people in the world of public education would definitely know. They would tell me and I could then get on to the question of how best to help schools achieve their mission.

Perhaps not surprisingly, I found there was no common definition or firm knowledge about the mission of school. Everyone had an opinion, but none was very specific nor of much help in providing clear direction for managing a school.

Many times I asked the question and received a blank stare. Sometimes I received an amused look. In some cases I was looked upon as being stupid for asking a question to which everyone supposedly knew the answer. In other cases, I received a variety of pat answers, such as:

- To educate children

- To prepare young people for life in the twenty-first century
- To prepare young people for the world of work

In one instance, a teacher told me the mission of school was, "to deliver the state-mandated curriculum to students."

In time it became obvious I was asking a question rarely asked by anyone. However, when pressed, even long-time educators had difficulty answering the question with any specificity and none of them came up with a response that was, in my mind, accurate or adequate.

The old adage, "if you don't know where you are going, any road will get you there" could apply to our schools. Because without agreeing on the mission of school, it is impossible to generate a plan to make schools effective and to have them achieve their intended purpose.

Most people believe the mission of school is to educate children. However, that is so obvious it does not really tell us anything. It's like saying the mission of business is to make a profit. Both sound correct, but neither is a true mission. Rather, educating children and making a profit are goals. Neither goal defines the real purpose of the organization, nor does either provide the people working in it with a clear understanding of why the organization exists. All businesses want to make a profit, but they exist for totally different reasons. For example, if the mission of business was to make a profit, then the missions of Apple, General Motors, Holiday Inn, and the corner dry cleaner would all be the same. Of course, each of these businesses has a different mission even though they all share the same goal of wanting to be profitable.

In the same way, if the mission of school is to "educate children," then that applies equally to K–12 schools, Sunday schools, community colleges, universities and the local karate studio. The term "educate children" does apply to all schools, but it is not a mission statement—it is a goal. It is also a goal of parents, or it should be. Moreover, what does it mean to "educate children?" What is an educated child?

Thus, the question stands: "What is the mission of school?" To answer that, one must first decide what the objective is and then decide what is required to meet that objective. A mission statement defines the purpose for an organization's existence. To be useful to the organization, the mission statement must be clear, concise, understood and committed to by the members of the organization.

Since no one gave me an answer that I found useful, I developed my own. I thought about the role of public schools in our society, and how schools relate to what I believe we need to achieve through the education of our young people. I looked at the history of our schools and tried to assess what might have worked in the past, what is working now, and what is not working now. How did we turn out a Jefferson or a Lincoln without compulsory public schools? What is it that a person needs to learn to be considered educated? What role does school have in turning out educated adults? These and other similar questions influenced my thinking in developing a mission statement for school.

If the goal of school is to turn out an educated child, then we must define such a child. In other words, we must define what an educated child should know and be able to do, and we should know when we have achieved the goal.

An Educated Child

IN 1992, the Secretary's Commission on Achieving Necessary Skills (SCANS) of the federal Department of Labor prepared a report on what young people would need to know and be able to do in order to be employable in the twenty-first century. That report suggested five mandatory skills. Those skills were the ability to:

- Manage resources
- Work with others
- Acquire and use information
- Understand systems

- Use technology[40]

Note: Some 20 years later, not a single state requires the mastery of even one of these skills in order to graduate from high school.

This list was perhaps influenced by an insightful article in *Fortune Magazine* (January 22, 1992), in which the authors suggested that an educated child would need to have:

- An ability to communicate effectively, orally and in writing

- A thorough grounding in literature and the social sciences, especially history and geography

- An understanding of the principles of higher mathematics, including the ability to apply those principles to daily life

- Knowledge of the physical sciences, including how these disciplines relate to the environment

- Mastery of at least one foreign language and culture

- Enough familiarity with computers and other technology to retrieve and use information easily

- An appreciation for the fine arts

- A genuine understanding of how the U.S. government and economy function

- Concern for physical health

- Above all else, the ability to identify problems and work creatively toward solutions[41]

A few years later, Howard Gardner in his book *Globalization: Culture and Education in the New Millennium* suggested seven skills needed for life in the twenty-first century. Those skills include an ability to:

- Understand global systems

- Think analytically and creatively within disciplines

---

40. Department of Labor, *Secretary's Report on Necessary Skills* (1992).
41. Kenneth Labich, "What Our Kids Must Learn," *Fortune Magazine* (January 27, 1992), 64–66.

- Tackle problems and issues that do not respect disciplinary boundaries
- Interact civilly and productively with individuals from different backgrounds—both within one's society and across the world
- Understand and respect their own cultural traditions
- Foster hybrid or blended identities—the ability to work, think and play across cultural boundaries
- Foster tolerance within and across nations[42]

The above lists of skills represent some good thinking. The *Fortune Magazine* list strikes me as being the best and most complete. It delineates what a child would need to learn to be considered a well-educated person. Education scholars have updated and expanded this list to emphasize skills they deem important in this age of global commerce, but they tend to agree on key details. Based upon their scholarship and my own observations, I have developed the following list. Here is what I think a high school graduate needs to know and be able to do to be considered educated. The graduate must have:

- Communication skills:
  - Is able to read, write and speak the English language
  - Is able to use technology to acquire and use information
- Citizenship skills:
  - Has an understanding of this country's history and the Constitution, has an appreciation of the right to vote, and intends to exercise that right
  - Has a basic understanding of economics and of how our economy works
- Global skills:
  - Has studied another language and culture

---

42. Howard Gardner, *Globalization: Culture and Education in the New Millennium* (Berkeley: University of California Press, 2004), 23–24.

- Has a reasonable understanding of world geography
- Math and science skills:
  - Can use and apply mathematical skills in daily life
  - Has an understanding of the physical sciences
- Personal qualities:
  - Does not lie, cheat or steal
  - Appreciates the needs of others
  - Is understanding of differing viewpoints
  - Has a good work ethic
  - Takes responsibility for his or her own actions
  - Has an understanding of the human body and how to live a healthy life

David Brooks, in his book *The Social Animal* asserts that *character* is a quality critical to the successful living of life. He describes people with character as being: "energetic, honest and dependable. They were persistent after setback and acknowledged their mistakes. They possessed enough integrity to live up to their commitments. They tried to recognize their weaknesses, atone for their sins, and control their worst impulses."[43]

I like Brooks' definition and feel it is a good description of the personal qualities needed to live a successful life in a civilized society. Willard Daggett further reinforces this point in his paper on "Addressing the Issue of Character." There he notes:

Whether we look at the basic characteristics of good citizenship from a democratic, religious, cultural or social/economic perspective, the same set of guiding principles keeps manifesting itself. Respect, responsibility, trustworthiness, loyalty, honesty, compassion, perseverance, courage, deliberateness, initiative, optimism and adaptability are

---

43. David Brooks, *The Social Animal* (New York: Random House, 2011), 8.

all important qualities regardless of a person's gender or political, racial and religious convictions."[44]

Character education takes on even more importance when you look at the history of societies. As Lawrence W. Reed, President of the Foundation for Economic Education, states in his excellent article on the history of the Roman Empire:

> The paramount lesson of the Roman experience is actually not peculiar to Rome. It may be, in fact, the most universal lesson of all history: No people who have lost their character have kept their liberties.[45]

Brooks summarizes the discussion of character education by saying, "We are good at teaching technical skills, but when it comes to the most important things, like character, we have almost nothing to say."[46]

You will note there is nothing in my list of education skills and principles that relates to grade point averages or the number of degrees or letters that appear after a person's name. Society does not measure people that way, nor should it. Rather, society measures people based on character, on personality, on morals, on work ethic, on devotion to family, on patriotism, on civic-mindedness, and on overall preparedness for living in a civilized society.

Education provides preparation for life. It is about equipping a young person to live in our society and become a productive citizen. It is not about whether the child is good or bad at math or science, although those are important. It is about knowing how to live and to contribute, in the child's own way, to the betterment of our world.

A young person possessing the skills and attributes listed above is able to take care of himself or herself, is able to earn a living, will not be a burden on society and accepts accountability and responsibility for his

---

44. Willard R. Daggett, "School Reform," International Center for Leadership in Education, Inc. (1998), 2, http://www.arkansased.org/public/userfiles/Learning_Services/Curriculum%20and%20Instruction/Char%20Cent%20Teach/dagget.pdf.

45. Lawrence W. Reed, "Are We Rome," Foundation for Economic Education (2014), 4, http://www.fee.org/files/doclib/20130620_FEEAreWeRomeCover1V5.pdf.

46. David Brooks, *The Social Animal* (New York: Random House, 2011), 14.

or her behavior. Such a person can best be described as a responsible citizen. This being the case, then one of the missions of school is to turn out responsible citizens.

Who Has the Responsibility?

Who is primarily responsible for the education of a child? Common wisdom suggests the school. Whenever student performance fails to meet expectations, parents, other citizens, policy makers and the media first blame the schools, or teachers, or both. Schools definitely impact student performance, but they are not where the primary blame belongs.

In 1992, President George H. W. Bush held an Education Summit in Charlottesville, Virginia, which Bill Clinton chaired. The summit resulted in a report, "Goals 2000."[47] The report included an amazing statistic. It stated that, "between birth and age 18, a young person will spend 90 percent of his life somewhere other than in school."[48]

Initially I didn't believe this figure and so calculated it myself and came up with 89.7 percent. This profound statistic suggests that schools are only one component of a child's education, but they are not the most important component. The statistic shows that **the primary responsibility for the education of a child rests with the child's parents or guardians, not with the school.** It also shows that because parents and guardians have the primary responsibility for the education of their child, schools actually serve parents in the work of educating their child. **Expressed another way, parents are the true customers of schools.**

This reasoning is not common in public education, but it has long been recognized by private schools. Private school parents are not only the primary source of funding, they are also considered the primary teachers of children. Private school teachers and administrators know

---

47. Department of Labor, "Raising Standards for American Education" (1992), http://www.scribd.com/doc/143404039/National-Council-On-Education-Standards-and-Testing-Raising-Standards-for-American-Education.
48. Ibid., 2.

that without extensive parental involvement in a child's education, that child will struggle. Successful public schools have also figured this out.

Children who have no parents or have parents unable or unwilling to participate in their child's education must receive such nurturing from another caring adult. Sometimes that is a grandparent, a neighbor, a teacher or another who provides a positive daily influence on a child. Teachers in private boarding schools can fill this role, or they should. The involvement of a caring adult in a child's education is vital, and since schools only occupy 10 percent of a child's life, the caring adult's intervention can best be done at home. It is becoming increasingly obvious that no child can be adequately prepared for adulthood without the care, nurture and love of an involved adult.

If parents are the primary educators of children, then schools, to be successful, must engage parents. They must treat parents as customers/partners and encourage parental involvement both at school and in the home. This reality is borne out of any analysis of high-performing schools, whether private or public. You will almost never find a high-performing school that does not have an inordinate amount of parental involvement. Such schools encourage, even demand, such involvement because they recognize the vital importance of parental participation in student learning.

This reality dictates how schools and districts must operate. They must cater to parents, meet parental requirements, and become parent-friendly. Smart schools and districts are creating *parent rooms* in schools. These rooms are designated for—and only for—parents to use during their school visits. Successful schools set goals for parental involvement and keep track of such involvement. Even in poverty-stricken neighborhoods, successful schools are able to engage parents in ways that are truly amazing. I have visited schools where welfare mothers, living in tenement housing, spend long hours in their children's school and come to believe that their children can be successful and that they, as parents, play an important role in making that happen.

Parents have many other partners who share in their responsibility—family members, friends, neighbors, peers, churches, synagogues or mosques and, of course, schools. Of those, however, the primary partner is the school.

The Mission

THUS, MY definition of the mission of a school recognizes the role of parents and the need to educate the child beyond the area of academics. My definition of the mission of a school is:

To serve as the primary partner, with parents, in the total development of their child into a responsible citizen.

Implications

FROM THIS mission statement, the following conclusions become obvious:

- The customer of a school is the parent, not the child, a labor union or the government.
- Parental involvement is essential for the successful operation of a school and for the successful education of a child.
- Communication between parent and teacher is essential.
- Schools need to teach more than academics.
- Parents are the most important teachers of their child.

The above conclusions also show why neighborhood schools are so important. They are particularly important in urban neighborhoods where parents may not own a car and have difficulty becoming involved in their child's school if it is located a significant distance from the child's home.

Separation of parent and school by distance explains why mandatory busing, a social experiment, was unsuccessful. It failed, not because of racism (although race was certainly a factor), but because busing systematically removed parents from the education of their child and from involvement in their child's school.

I have come to the conclusion that the racial integration of our schools is really a question of the real estate market, not a social policy issue. There will always be concentrations of like people in specific neighborhoods. We saw that in various cities in the early years of our country's development. Italian people concentrated in one part of town, Irish people in another and Polish people in still another. Most major cities have a Chinatown. This is normal and predictable.

Today, we see Korean neighborhoods, Vietnamese neighborhoods, Hispanic neighborhoods, etc. We have always had African-American neighborhoods, part of which was due to past racism, but part due to a desire to live near people of like backgrounds. This concentration of similar people causes neighborhood schools to have concentrations of like types of students. This is to be expected and should not be discouraged or denied. Rather, parents must maintain control of where their child goes to school, and having that child as close to home as possible is beneficial to that child's education, particularly in the early grades. This belief will often yield highly concentrated populations of racially and/or ethnically similar children. Some call this the re-segregation of our schools. However, if a parent chooses the school closest to home and lives in a racially concentrated community, then that is not segregation. It is parental choice.

The important question is not, "Who is sitting next to my child in class?" but rather, "Is my child attending a quality school?" School districts, cities and the courts should spend more time improving the quality of all schools rather than managing the racial, ethnic or cultural makeup of particular student bodies. Also, total choice with a preference to the neighborhood school is, in my mind, the best type of "student assignment" policy.

Role of the Parent

SCHOOLS MUST have parental involvement if they are to be successful in achieving their mission. In one school I visited, there was a contract between the school and the parents. The school agreed to ensure that their child would perform at grade level or higher in every subject, if the parents agreed that the child would come to school well fed, clean, rested and adequately clothed, that the parents would attend meetings at the school as requested, and that they would perform at home those tasks requested of them by the teachers.

Parents were asked to commit to reading to their child every day for at least 20 minutes. This was an elementary school located in a low-income neighborhood. The population of the school was 80 percent minority students, and over 70 percent of the student body qualified for free or reduced lunches (the definition used in education to define poverty). The students did very well. There was high parental involvement and virtually no disciplinary problems.

Total Development

I SELECTED the term *total development* very carefully. Total development means the child is taught values, learns right from wrong, acquires self-confidence and can get along with others. The child also has a good work ethic, in addition to knowing math, science, English, reading, writing, and other subjects.

Total development cannot occur only in school, but it must be a part of school. Total development demands that the adults in school serve as excellent role models for the children. Teachers must help instill the traits needed for successful living. As we know, core habits of motivation, empathy, self-control and persistence are necessary for living in our society and are also key components in a child's ability to learn. Self-discipline is more important than IQ when it comes to academic performance.[49] Also, "conscientiousness—a tendency to be responsible, hard

---

49. Amanda Ripley, *The Smartest Kids in the World* (New York: Simon and Schuster, 2013), 120.

working, and organized—matters at every point in the human life cycle. It even predicts how long people will live—with more accuracy than intelligence or background."[50]

Responsible Citizen

THE TERM *responsible citizen* means that the child, upon graduation, is able to take care of himself or herself and will not become a burden to society. It means the child will enter adulthood capable of making a living or capable of continuing his or her formal education. It means that he or she recognizes personal ownership of behavior, self-management and creating success. A responsible citizen is an adult knowledgeable enough about our country's history, government, Constitution and economic system to be an informed voter. Finally, a responsible citizen is an adult capable of being a responsible parent.

Conclusion

IF WE, as a society, could instill in our young people the skills and character traits listed above, we would have an educated, responsible electorate. We would reduce poverty and crime, and our country would become extraordinarily competitive in world markets. Our government would operate more effectively and efficiently, because there would be far fewer people dependent upon the social safety-net services provided by government.

This mission statement suggests that our schools should operate differently than they do today. Not only must schools recognize their role in the total development of a child, they must recognize the role of parents and of the community. They must be attuned to meeting the requirements of both the parents and the child. They must give parents greater opportunity and responsibility to be involved in their children's education.

Schools should become community learning centers where not only the child but also the parents and members of the community can gather

---

50. Ibid., 123.

to learn and to participate in the total development of the child. School employees must model behavior and structure that will enhance the total development of the child. Teachers and administrators need to understand that their role extends far beyond teaching a subject; they need to be teachers about life. They need to be role models in everything they do.

In summary, the mission of school can provide the very foundation upon which our society can be improved and rebuilt. It is obvious that our society has many problems today at all levels. It is equally obvious that the trouble starts early in life and continues from one generation to another. If we can get back to basics by promoting personal accountability and by teaching strong character traits to our young people, in addition to academics, a multitude of other social ills will start to heal. Understanding the mission of school is the key starting point.

4.

Unions and Change

Unions are often criticized as the biggest obstacle to bringing real change in America's public schools. That criticism is largely justified. There are many cities in this country where the union leadership is much more interested in holding power than in educating children. However, asking unions to change is like asking water to flow uphill. Unions abhor change and will fight it with all the power they have, and they have a lot of power.

However, they did not start out as a powerful entity. Unions derive their power from weak management. In fact, unions' strong position is the result of management failure. One need only look at the history of the labor movement, at any industry where it is strong, to find workers who felt a need to organize in order to obtain reasonable wages, fair treatment and better working conditions. As workers, teachers are no different.

The bigger question is, how do we create an environment where unions and management can work together? How can we mitigate the power of unions and/or how do we develop a school system where teachers are not forced, or don't feel a need, to belong to a union?

For the first half of the twentieth century, the power over schools rested with the administrators and school boards. Teachers had little say and were not organized in any way. In those days, teaching was the primary employment opportunity for women. Some teachers were treated well, and some were not. Compensation was quite variable, as were work-

ing conditions. After WWII, as unions gained strength in other industries, teachers began to organize. In the 1960s, this was made easier as
both states and the federal government enacted laws that allowed, and in
some cases encouraged, public employees to engage in collective bargaining. Terry Moe writes, "By the time the dust settled in the early 1980s,
virtually all districts of any size (outside the South) were successfully
organized, collective bargaining was the norm, and the teachers unions
reigned supreme as the most powerful force in American education."[51]

Over the years, unions have been successful in raising teacher compensation, improving teacher working conditions, and protecting teacher employment. That is their job and they do it well. However, in protecting the economic interests of teachers, they have handcuffed effective
managers, blocked positive change, and resolutely preserved the status
quo. They have done this so well, in fact, that public education has seen
little meaningful reform in the last 30 years.

Since 1980, union membership has grown fastest in the public sector. A large portion of city, county, state and federal workers across the
country are now members of collective bargaining units. Public education, as an arm of government, fits into this category. Today, even in
"Right to Work" states, education unions are powerful elements of the
education workforce. Unions, as one would expect, are strongest where
management has been weakest and most compliant.

Conversely, unions have declined dramatically in the private sector.
In private companies, managers have become more sophisticated and
more conscious that taking care of employees is as important as taking
care of their customers. In fact, one concern begets the other. Wherever
you see excellent managers, you will generally see weak unions or no
unions at all. Workers, in a well-managed organization, do not need a
union in order to have good working conditions, competitive compensation and job security. However, a well-managed organization provides

---

51. Terry Moe, "The Staggering Power of Teachers' Unions," *Hoover Digest* no. 3 (2011), 94,
   http://www.hoover.org/research/staggering-power-teachers-unions.

those conditions only when performance by the worker is satisfactory. In these type of organizations, there is no protection for incompetence, nor is there a seniority-based guarantee of employment. Employees in these organizations must continue to contribute in order to maintain their positions.

Public education does not work that way, but it should. Today, teachers and principals often receive tenure after only three years on the job. Once tenure is achieved, it becomes very difficult to dismiss a teacher or principal, regardless of inability to perform their job. This situation perpetuates mediocrity, which hurts the education of children.

Joel Klein, former chancellor of the New York City Schools, described union effectiveness this way:

> [U]nion members... want lifetime job security (tenure), better pay regardless of performance (seniority pay), less work (short days, long holidays, lots of sick days), and the opportunity to retire early (at say, 55) with a good lifetime pension and full health benefits; for their part, the retirees want to make sure their benefits keep coming and grow through cost-of-living increases. The result: whether you work hard or don't, get good results with kids or don't, teach in a shortage area like math or special education or don't, or in a hard-to-staff school in a poor community or not, you get paid the same, unless you've been around for another year, in which case you get more. Not bad for adults... disastrous for kids in our schools.[52]

Some years ago, I had lunch with the president of the state-level teachers' union in Washington state, the Washington Education Association (WEA). During our lunch, I asked her, "What is the mission of the union?" She was somewhat taken aback by the question, but said, "The mission of the union is the education of children." I told her I disagreed. We discussed the issue for over an hour, and when we finished, she agreed that the mission of the union was:

---

52. Joel Klein, "The Failure of American Schools," *The Atlantic Monthly* (June, 2011), 2, http://www.theatlantic.com/magazine/archive/2011/06/the-failure-of-american-schools/308497/.

- To maximize teacher pay.

- To improve teachers' working conditions.

- To secure and protect teacher employment.

I agreed with that definition of her union's mission. I also agreed that they had done a magnificent job of achieving their mission, but it was done at the expense of our children. Even though the union has been successful in achieving their mission, I pointed out that it was the wrong mission. I said that because there is increasing concern about the performance of our schools and their ability to educate our children. Test scores have not changed, drop-out rates have not changed, and the achievement gap (the difference in test scores between whites and minorities) has not changed. Pressure to reform the system is escalating and will not subside until progress is made. So I suggested to her that until and unless the union focuses on furthering the interests of children, not adults, it would be unsuccessful in effectively educating every child, which is what their mission should be. What it should do, as an organization, is focus on the teaching effectiveness of every union member to ensure the effective education of every child. If they did that, the union could achieve its mission on behalf of its members. High-performing schools attract students, and that increases the number of teachers, which in turn, increases union membership and dues.

The three elements of the union mission described above all focused on the needs and desires of adults, while public schools need to focus on ensuring that children learn. Thus, there is an inherent conflict that arises every time union representatives and school managers gather to negotiate. The union negotiators focus on the needs or perceived needs of its members, and school managers must focus on the needs of parents and students, who are their customers.

School managers also need to be concerned about the needs of employees in order to be successful at meeting customer requirements. When that occurs, the organization flourishes. When it doesn't occur, you see strong unions and, more often than not, poor-quality education for children.

This tension plays out in public schools and in government agencies. You also saw it in the automobile industry. Auto manufacturing, which is one of the most heavily unionized industries in our country, had some of the most worker-focused contracts ever negotiated. However, those labor contracts could not protect the workers from marketplace competition as car buyers found they could buy a better car and/or a less-expensive car from foreign manufacturers. The result was a rapid decline in the size and market share of domestic manufacturers. Today, the United Auto Workers (UAW) has 600,000 fewer members than it had in the 1980s. Schools are witnessing the same trend, as private and charter schools grow and take market share from public schools. This trend will continue unless public school managers and local unions focus on their customers—parents and students.

Over the decades, public school teachers unions have been able to secure extensive management concessions, strict grievance procedures, generous sick leave and union leave provisions, rich benefit packages, stringent work rules and tenure. In most cases, these broad economic entitlements for adults have dramatically increased the cost of operating public schools—thereby alienating taxpayers—and have not enhanced student academic achievement. These economic gains were conceded by weak management and by the increasing power of the unions. Contract terms, over the years, have been built upon until they have become a major constraint to the effective operation of schools.

A report by the *Education Partnership* (March 2005), points out that union contracts have now arrived at a point where they consistently:

- Restrict flexibility and school autonomy
- Drive up the cost of education without improving quality

- Entrench the role of the union position in labor contracts, weakening management rights[53]

They further state that union contracts are filled with:

the micromanagement of teachers, limitations to instructional time, generous paid time-off, incredible health and retirement packages, teacher transfer and assignment rights, limits to evaluation of teachers and numerous other stipulations. Many of these contract mandates limit the ability of teachers to perform as professionals and serve their students, and the authority of administrators to get the most out of the public's education dollars.[54]

Weak management deserves a strong union, but as management improves, contract terms become a constraint in improving the operation of any organization, including public schools. The base union contract for Seattle Public Schools is 157 pages long and its terms reflect decades of mistrust. It is the most limiting and onerous employment agreement I have ever read. The table of contents of the current contract is attached as Exhibit A and will provide you with an overview of the complexity of this employment agreement. This contract is not dissimilar to contracts in other urban school systems of this country.

As we endeavor to improve our schools, the dominant position of unions within public education must change. However, you cannot expect unions to lead this change, as their job is to protect the interests, compensation and employment of their members. Union leaders will not willingly give up hard-won provisions of a labor contract.

Nor can superintendents or school boards expect a local union to support change just because they believe it to be in the best interest of children. Rather, school boards and superintendents must first regain trust from the district employees and the community at large. This requires excellent people in both positions. Without effective leadership and stable governance, unions not only will continue to resist change,

---

53. "Teacher Contracts: Restoring the Balance," Executive Summary, *The Education Partnership* (March 2005), 7.
54. Ibid., 7.

they are in a position to ensure that reform decisions made by management are not implemented.

Implementing change will require leadership that gains not only the trust of public education employees and of the community, but also of union leadership. That can be difficult because management and unions are seldom in agreement on any substantive issue. Management generally wants more production for less money, and unions want more money for less work. It is a built-in conflict. The problem is also obvious, however, and, therefore, can be dealt with.

The best example I can give of how change can be made, even with a strong union, is the experience of Seattle in 1996–97. In September of 1995, while serving on the school board, my colleagues and I had appointed John Stanford, a former Army major general, as superintendent. One of his first initiatives was to connect personally with the teachers employed by the District. He would visit area schools every morning, four days a week. He was the first superintendent to visit all 96 of Seattle's public schools in one year. His visits included not only meeting with the principal, but also visiting classrooms, where he would talk with and listen to teachers. He would empathize with them over the daily challenges they faced and promised to work to correct problems. He also connected with the children. He urged them to work hard, to listen to their teachers, to come to school every day and to strive to do their best. This personal concern for students endeared him to parents as well.

As Superintendent Stanford toured area schools, he discussed with union representatives ways to improve teacher performance. He wanted union leaders to know he was concerned about ensuring every child was taught by a competent teacher. For their part, union leaders felt the problem faced by teachers was more about principal competency than about teacher performance. The union's concern was to protect its members from the unfair decisions of incompetent principals. For this reason a serious impasse developed.

Superintendent Stanford, who expected the same high performance from principals as he did from teachers, decided to invite the union to become a partner with school district management in improving the quality of all employees—teachers, principals, support staff, and others.

Washington State is one of the most heavily unionized states in the country. Unions hold political power at all levels of government, and they fight any and all efforts to reduce their dominant status. Given this situation, it was obvious that the only way to bring positive change to schools, at the district level, was to do so in concert with the union and not attempt to force change against organized labor's wishes. Stanford and the board felt we could not succeed in this effort without the union's concurrence.

At the time of Superintendent Stanford's appointment, principals in Seattle Public Schools exercised no authority over staff, money or curriculum. They were, however, expected to be accountable to the public and to the school board for the educational performance of their schools. It was an impossible situation, and both Superintendent Stanford and we, on the school board, knew it. We felt each local principal, in order to be professionally accountable to us, needed to have staffing authority, budgetary authority and operational authority over his or her own school.

With such authority granted locally, the superintendent would be in a position to measure the effectiveness of each principal and could then weed out incompetent managers. We decided that we first had to improve the professional competence of principals before we could set accountability expectations for teachers. To make that happen, we had to change the job description of the principal by building in local accountability for staff selection and performance, budget preparation, spending and student learning. This required a change in the union contract, with regard to staffing rules and a change in how we allocated money to schools. Superintendent Stanford, with the blessing of the school board, approached the union with a plan.

Our proposal was that the school district would agree to get rid of incompetent principals, in return for union support in bringing about needed change. To do that, we recognized the need to have the principal job be modified so they had specific accountability over the performance of their building. This meant principals had to be given authority over staff, over the expenditure of money, and over the rules for operating their building.

The union was very supportive of management's intention to dismiss incompetent principals and supported that effort. Union leaders understood that, in order for principals to be accountable, principals needed to be given the level of the authority we proposed. Thus, the issue of employee seniority came immediately to the forefront of our discussions. If we were to give our principals authority to hire the teachers they wanted, they could not continue to be obligated to hire blindly on the basis of teacher seniority. Obviously, the union was against this proposal. Teacher seniority is a sacred job security policy of unions, and for them to give it up would be to act against everything they stood for.

The district was adamant that seniority rules had to be relaxed in order to create accountability for principals, which itself was a prerequisite to management's being able to terminate incompetent principals. The union was equally adamant that seniority was a job-protection rule they could not give up. The two parties were at an impasse.

After much frank negotiating, however, and the establishment of trust between management and the union, an agreement was reached that worked for both parties. The union agreed to eliminate seniority as the basis for hiring teachers, in exchange for the creation of a *leadership team* in each building. In practice, each school would create a leadership team made up of six employees working in the building, elected by their peers. This team of six people would work with the principal in the selection and hiring of new teaching staff, in setting rules for the daily operation of the building and in the preparation of the school budget. The board and superintendent agreed to this provision provided the final decision on all these matters would rest with the principal. The union reluctantly agreed!

A new contract was prepared and signed by union representatives and district management. This was a landmark achievement, and three years later, when the labor contract was up for renewal, the issue of seniority in hiring was not even a subject of discussion. In the intervening three years, the leadership team concept had worked so well that teachers in each school wanted to retain their new authority. They obviously liked being able to help select the people with whom they would work.

From the principal's point of view, the arrangement made managing daily operations easier and more effective. More of the teaching staff was involved in making key decisions, and staff competence improved along with staff morale. It was a true win-win situation. This agreement took place in 1997. As far as I can determine, Seattle is still one of the few urban districts in the country where principals exercise staffing authority over their own school.

The above experience is a classic example of how effective school district management can work with unions to initiate change. A successful process starts with trust, and then requires agreement on a common outcome. In this case, the union wanted the district to rid itself of incompetent principals (no principal had been fired in the previous 25 years) and the district wanted to change the job of the principal so it would encompass the accountability needed to evaluate performance and, if necessary, terminate incompetent principals. The net effect of the new union agreement was the dismissal of four principals, followed by that of three other principals the following year.

In addition, many principals decided to retire or transfer to other school districts rather than be held accountable for their school's performance. Conversely, principals from all over the country started applying to work in Seattle Public Schools. Over a period of the five years, following the ratification of this new contract, the school district replaced 70 of the 96 principals in the district. After these changes had occurred, the union had very few complaints about the competency of the leadership working in school buildings.

Not only was the school district able to upgrade the quality of principals, but principals in turn dramatically improved the quality of teachers working in the schools. Really good principals will not tolerate incompetent teachers. Nor will they tolerate good teachers unwilling to advance the goals and plans managers adopt to help students. Thus, a number of teachers were dismissed. Also, many teachers left the district, or transferred to schools within the district where their particular approach to teaching was more compatible with the manner in which that school was being operated. Again, the voluntary movement of teaching personnel created a win-win situation for the school employees, for the students and for public education.

This change in the contract allowed the union to achieve some of its goals as well. Working conditions improved for the teachers. Local schools received new and better leaders, teachers had more input to how the school operated, and staff morale improved.

Children also benefited as the schools began to operate more effectively. This resulted in increased test scores, reduced drop-out rates and a dramatic decrease in violence and disruptions. Also, the voters started passing levies that had formerly been defeated. The ultimate impact was an increase in the student population of the district, as parents began to believe in Seattle Public Schools again. The net effect was the hiring of more teachers to handle increased enrollment (thus increasing union membership and dues), another win for the union.

I should point out that one of the reasons all this occurred was because of the charismatic leadership of Superintendent John Stanford. He had practically become a folk hero in Seattle, and the public was behind virtually anything he wanted to do. The union knew this and knew that if John Stanford felt he needed to eliminate seniority in the hiring of teachers, and if he went to the public with that issue, the public would very likely support him and not the union. Even though the solution was a win-win for the union and the district, I believe it would not have happened without truly competent leadership at the superintendent level and at the board level.

Between 1968 and the early 1990s, Seattle Public Schools dropped in enrollment from 100,000 children to 39,000. Today, there are almost 50,000 students attending public schools in Seattle. That earlier drop in student enrollment reduced teacher employment by over 4,000. It also reduced union membership by the same amount. When a union loses members, it loses dues revenue. In other words, contracted job security cannot be accomplished in education any more than it could in the automobile industry.

Job security is accomplished only by meeting customer (parents and students) requirements. As schools improve, parents will bring their children back to the district. Not only are teachers retained, but new ones are hired, and everyone in the system achieves their goals—including the economic goals of the union. In Seattle, our union leaders understood this reality, and, once they did, a partnership was established that has helped the district, the union and the students of Seattle succeed.

A subscript to this story is the sad and early death of John Stanford due to cancer. He was a dynamic leader, and, without a similar leader, the district again went into decline. Within less than five years of his passing in November of 1998, the district became embroiled in a crippling financial scandal, the voters elected a new, activist board, the succeeding superintendent was removed and trust between the school system and the public began to wane. Over the following ten years, the district experienced five superintendents, high turnover in school board membership and variable and unstable support from parents. By the early 2000s, student enrollment had again declined and is only now starting to recover. In 2011, seven public schools were closed amid much community acrimony. In 2014, district relations with the teachers union can be described as only fair.

The difficulty of maintaining reform is not unique to Seattle. It happens time and again in communities throughout the country. In fact, few urban districts have been able to sustain a long-term effort for school improvement. Education leaders in New York, Boston and Chicago are trying, but with only limited success so far. Even when effective leadership is present, change is not sustainable, because dynamic leaders move on, but the local union remains. Washington, D.C., under the leadership of Michelle Rhee, was the most aggressive at changing the system, but her constructive reforms were soon stopped by the union's ability to unseat her political protector, Mayor Fantey.

Over the years, union power has substantially increased to the point where it now influences elections at the national, state and local levels. Today, labor unions have more influence on the public schools than any other group in American society, including voters.[55] As education policy analyst Terry Moe puts it:

> Their influence takes two forms. They shape schools from the bottom up, through collective bargaining activities so broad in scope that virtually every aspect of school organization bears the distinctive imprint of union design. They also shape the schools from the top down, through political activities that give them unrivaled influence over the laws and regulations imposed on public education by Government, that allow them to block or weaken governmental reforms they find threatening. In combining bottom-up and top-down influence, and in combining them as potently as they do, the teachers unions are unique among all actors in the educational area.[56]

Unions have an additional advantage unique to education. Because all districts are mandated to provide 180 days of schooling per year, the threat of a strike does not incur any economic disadvantage to teachers. If they go on strike, the school year is simply extended. Thus, there is no penalty to the worker as there is in other industries. Also, a strike quickly alienates the parent community, who almost immediately put

---

55. Terry Moe, "The Staggering Power of Teachers' Unions," *Hoover Digest* 3 (Summer 2011), 94, http://www.hoover.org/research/staggering-power-teachers-unions.
56. Ibid.

pressure on school boards to settle any dispute. These two factors give unions enormous power over school management.

Today, the National Education Association (NEA) is the largest union in the country and has the most influence on political races throughout the nation. Combined with the American Federation of Teachers (AFT), the two labor organizations have a combined membership of "well over 4 million."[57]

In the twenty-year period 1989–2010, these two unions were the largest political contributors to candidates in federal elections.[58] They are also powerful contributors in local and state elections and, as can be seen in almost any city, can strongly influence, and almost determine, the outcome of local school board elections. In fact, these two unions can and have influenced elections at every level of public office, and, as long as they retain their power, every indication is they will continue to do so.

The bottom line is that the opposition of teachers unions is a major force to contend with in the ongoing effort to improve our public schools. They know their mission and they carry it out admirably. If we are serious about fixing our public schools, we will have to ultimately deal with the power of unions, but that can only occur after we have improved the competency of education management, not only at the school and district level, but at the state level as well.

This whole process of reform must start with effective leadership and the rebuilding of trust. Without trust, nothing can occur; with it, anything is possible.

There is no question unions impose a major constraint on efforts to improve our schools, but that constraint can be accommodated if there is effective leadership at the principal, superintendent and board levels of management. Permanently reducing the negative impact of unions on the effective education of our children can occur only through a radical

---

57. Terry Moe, *Special Interest: Teachers Unions and America's Public Schools* (Washington, DC: Brookings Institution Press, 2011), 8.
58. Ibid., 283.

increase in the competency of leadership in our schools, cities and states. Working on improving leadership first is a basic requirement of mitigating union opposition to constructive change.

Recently, we have seen the power of leadership exercised at the state level, particularly in Wisconsin and Indiana. Governors Scott Walker and Mitch Daniels have exercised enormous leadership related to unions. Daniels managed to pass a Right To Work law in Indiana, and Walker has managed to remove mandated union membership for government employees. This latter move has allowed schools in Wisconsin to become the equivalent of charter schools, as each school is now free to hire only the best teachers and reward excellence in teaching, if they so choose. The net effect is that education costs have declined, schools have improved and both the parents and taxpayers have come out ahead. In addition, I am certain that the teachers are finding their new freedom invigorating. Again, fixing leadership is the primary way to combat the power of unions.

Sometimes it can be necessary to use other means to combat the power of unions. The very recent (June 2014) court ruling in *Vergara v. California* is an example where the courts can be helpful in reducing the power of unions. This case pertained to the right of students to have access to quality teachers. Nine students filed the case to overturn the seniority and tenure laws that offer job security to educators. Their contention was that these laws prevented them from having equal access to quality teachers. The court agreed with their argument and ruled both laws unconstitutional, a huge win for students, for parents and for quality teachers.

This is a landmark decision that will have ramifications well beyond the State of California. More state legislatures will be looking at seniority and tenure as questionable contract terms and assessing their impact on student achievement. By giving principals more discretion in the hiring and retention of teachers, it becomes even more important that we immediately work on improving the leadership in education, as quality teachers are going to demand quality leadership.

However, even the elimination of seniority and tenure will not totally diffuse the power of unions. They are still going to wield tremendous power that will continue to handcuff our school systems. This court decision will cause them to work even harder to solidify their position. As a consequence, effective leadership becomes even more essential. Improving the quality of management and leadership of our schools and of our state governments is still an essential step in improving our schools. Though unions are, in my mind, the major constraint to improving our schools, they are not the source of the problem—management is! And here, management refers not only to school and district management, but to state and federal management as well. Leadership needs to improve at all levels and laws need to be changed before we can hope to diminish the power of unions.

PART TWO:

STEPS FOR CHANGE

5.

TEACHING

IN MANY OF MY SPEECHES ON EDUCATION, I WOULD START BY ASKING a question: "How many of you can recall one teacher who made a positive difference in your education and, perhaps, in the person you have become?" Almost every hand in the room would go up. I would then ask, "How many of you can remember two teachers who made a positive difference in your life?" About half the hands would go up. I would then ask, "How many of you can recall three such teachers?" About 10 percent of the hands would go up.

What is interesting about this is that, in our K–12 schooling years, each of us probably had 30 to 35 teachers. In other words, most of us cannot remember or were not materially influenced by over 90 percent of the teachers we had in school. This is a pretty sad statistic, but it is the way school was for most of us. This may say something about our poor memories, but it says far more about the quality of our teachers. When we were fortunate enough to be assigned to a gifted teacher, that person positively influenced us, often for life.

No matter how many research papers you read about teaching, the one universal truth is that quality teaching yields quality learning for students. Studies have shown that if you take high-performing students and put them in a classroom with a low-performing teacher, they will soon become low-performing students. Conversely, if you put low performing students in a classroom with a high-performing teacher, they will become high-performing students. Parents matter most, but then teachers. [59]

Kati Haycock of the Education Trust says, "A decade ago... we believed that what students learned was largely a factor of their family income or parental education, not of what schools did. But recent research has turned these assumptions upside down. What schools do matters— enormously. And what matters most, is good teaching."[60] In other words, how well a child learns in school is primarily determined by the quality of the teacher in the classroom.

Data tells us that a quality teacher can overcome the effects on students of a poor home environment. A good teacher can allow a child to succeed in class, in spite of the social and economic circumstances into which the child was born.

Great teachers can make miracles happen. They are, perhaps, the most important members of our society. When students receive excellent teaching, year after year, they flourish. If a student receives poor teaching for only a few years, that child's education will be permanently damaged. This point is corroborated by research done in Tennessee schools that showed a fourfold increase in learning achievement by students who had a series of excellent teachers compared to students of similar backgrounds who had a series of poor teachers.[61]

Poor-quality teaching or inadequate teaching has a huge economic impact as well. Universities and community colleges have to provide hours of remedial classes for a large percentage of their entering students. Businesses suffer by not having available the trained people needed to staff their operations. Our overall prosperity suffers, and the cost to the economy runs into billions of dollars.[62]

59. "How to Be Top," *The Economist* (October 20, 2007), 80.
60. Kati Haycock, "Closing the Achievement Gap," *Educational Leadership* (March 2001).
61. "Good Teaching Matters—How Well-Qualified Teachers Can Close the Gap," *Thinking K–16* 3, no. 2 (Washington, DC: Education Trust, 1998), 3–5.
62. Jay P. Greene, The Cost of Remedial Education: How Much Michigan Pays When Students Fail to Learn Basic Skills" (Midland, MI: MacKinac Center for Public Policy, 2003), 3.

Eric Hanushek, of Stanford University's Hoover Institution, estimates that a significant improvement in education, over a 20-year period, could lead to as much as a four percentage point boost in the Gross Domestic Product. In today's terms, that would be over $800 billion in economic growth a year, an amount that rivals total current spending on K–12 public education.

The future of this country depends on our having a well-educated citizenry. To make that a reality, we must have excellent schools available to all children. As one respected national report put it, "Top-quality teaching fosters high student achievement—and high achievers can harness their talents and energies to become successful, contributing citizens."[63]

Given the validity of that statement, it would seem reasonable to expect a country to treat teaching as a high-status profession. Yet, here in America, we do anything but. We continue to "treat teaching – the profession that makes all other professions possible – as a second-rate occupation."[64]

The Education Trust puts it this way:

> Nearly 200,000 graduates from schools of education and those who have completed alternative route teaching programs are placed in American classrooms each year. Too often, these educators and the school districts that hire them find out all too soon that they are ill prepared for the demands of today's classrooms. As a consequence, the children in their classes do not have the opportunity to learn to high levels. This practice is unfair to teachers and devastating to students, especially to students of color, low-income students, English language learners, and students with disabilities, who year after year are taught by the least effective teachers.[65]

---

63. The Teaching Commission, "Teaching At Risk, A Call to Action," (2004), 12.
64. Ibid. 10.
65. "Joint Statement from Twelve Education Organizations on the U.S. Department of Education's Teacher Preparation Regulation" (April 25, 2014), http://www.edtrust.org/dc/press-room/news/joint-statement-from-twelve-education-organizations-on-the-us-department-of-educa.

The lack of emphasis on teaching is one of the reasons our children are not performing at levels that are competitive with other countries. Though substantial increases in funding of education have occurred in the past several decades, student test scores are still about the levels they were in 1970. Moreover, we face a significant ethnicity gap. The Education Trust reports that 33 of every 100 white students who enter kindergarten will graduate from college, but only 18 of every 100 African-American kindergartners will earn a similar degree. Hispanic children have comparable statistics.[66] An increasing number of today's jobs require at least a two-year advanced degree in order for an applicant to qualify for a position. The above dismal performance, for white, black and Hispanic students does not come close to meeting the demands of society. If the level of learning cannot be increased, this country will rapidly lose its position as a world economic leader and the standard of living for our citizens will decline. This prediction is already coming true for an increasing number of our citizens.

The quality of teaching matters! In fact, all other factors pale in comparison. So how are we doing in attracting and retaining excellent teachers?

Today, a third of teachers entering the profession will leave before they complete their fifth year in the classroom. In large urban systems, fully half of teachers will leave within five years. In some of those districts, half leave within three years.[67] Moreover, the first teachers to leave the profession tend to be those who had the best SAT scores when entering university.[68] Though a high SAT score is not a guarantee of teaching success, it is a good indicator of a person's verbal and cognitive skills. Studies show that teachers with strong verbal and cognitive ability are

---

66. Education Trust, "Good Teaching Matters—How Well-Qualified Teachers Can Close the Gap," *Thinking K–16* 3, no. 2 (Washington, DC: Education Trust, 1998), 4.
67. The Teaching Commission, "Teaching at Risk: A Call to Action" (2004), 19.
68. National Commission on Teaching and America's Future, "No Dream Denied: Pledge to America's Children, Summary Report" (Washington, D.C.: NCTAF, 2003), 13.

most likely to improve student achievement.[69] In fact, a teacher's verbal and cognitive ability has a greater impact on student learning than any other measured characteristic.[70]

The departure of large numbers of teachers, particularly the brightest, has created a competency crisis in our schools. This crisis will only get worse over the next decade, because our country will need to add two million new teachers, almost half of whom will be needed in urban areas.

So we have a national situation in which the most important profession in our society is experiencing high turnover, and is losing its best people the fastest. Moreover, the vast majority of our best and brightest people don't even consider entering the profession of teaching.

Some would argue that the reason the best and brightest young people do not seek to become teachers is the amount of money we pay our teachers. I'm sure that is one consideration, but later I will discuss teacher compensation and why it is not the overriding reason our brightest people do not enter the profession. I would argue that we have so few gifted teachers partly because of the many new career opportunities now open to women, but primarily because of the restrictive laws and regulations governing teaching that make it an unattractive profession.

Getting the best teachers requires that we encourage the best students from our universities and the best people from our society to go into teaching. That does not occur in our present education system. Richard Elmore puts it this way; "Today, we have a cartel that controls the supply of human capital that is allowed into our schools. This cartel consists of 'state agencies, cash-for-credit university programs and hopelessly inadequate local hiring practices.'"[71]

To overcome these problems and improve the quality of our teaching corps, we must address three issues:

---

69. Grover Whitehurst, "Raising Student Achievement: The Evidence of High Quality Teaching," remarks at STEP 2002 Summer Conference (June 11, 2002).
70. The Teaching Commission, "Teaching At Risk: A Call to Action" (2004), 18.
71. Richard F. Elmore, "Breaking the Cartel," *Phi Delta Kappan* (March 2006), 517, http://www.kappanmagazine.org/content/87/7/517.abstract.

1. Selection and Preparation

2. Placement and Working Conditions

3. Compensation

All three areas require major changes if we truly expect to make teaching a real profession and to have our brightest citizens enter and spend at least several years in the teaching field.

1. Selection and Preparation

PROFESSIONALS IN areas of law, medicine, engineering, etc., are carefully selected prior to being accepted into a college program. They then go through extensive educational training followed by on-the-job training. New lawyers come into law firms and work directly under a partner or other experienced lawyer. Doctors graduate from medical school and serve an extensive internship prior to practicing medicine on their own. Engineers join an engineering firm, continue their training and then take an exam to get licensed. Certified public accountants do much the same. Professors in universities conduct extensive study in their area of expertise before applying for faculty positions. Would-be professors must prove they possess a deep knowledge of a subject area and have an ability to teach it effectively to college students.

In each case, the individual is carefully selected (only the best and brightest are accepted) and must receive extensive training beyond the classroom to prove qualification before being allowed to practice.

However, entry into teaching is not done that way. All a teacher-to-be has to do is get accepted into an education school, which is the easiest college on a campus to get into, and then complete the curriculum required of the chosen school of education. This rather bizarre reality is the result of our state teacher-certification laws. The narrow cartel mentioned above is the direct result of these restrictive laws. Certification laws were supposedly designed to ensure that only "qualified" teachers entered our classrooms. Requiring that teachers be officially certified, it was argued, would ensure that only high-quality instruction was allowed in the classroom. Today, however, these well-intentioned laws are a large stumbling block to real improvement in our teaching force.

These laws required the creation of schools of education at universities and colleges throughout the country. Education schools were established for the purpose of developing the art and science of teaching. Professors for these schools would be drawn from other disciplines of the university. Graduates of these schools would then be "certified" teachers thoroughly familiar with their subject area and competent to teach it.

Initially, schools of education were well staffed and the professional training they provided was on a par with other academic disciplines within the university.

In addition to the formation of schools of education, state certification laws mandated that public school administrators could hire only officially certified teachers, that is, those who had attended and completed the course of study at an approved school of education. I am sure, that in the early years, this requirement was useful in improving the teaching profession. However, today that is no longer the case.

Laws that mandated the hiring of only certified teachers resulted in giving schools of education monopoly control over the supply of human capital entering our public schools. Like any monopoly, over time the business of certifying teachers became bureaucratized, bloated, inefficient and ineffective. Today, there are over 1,400 schools that are licensed to grant teacher certifications.

In most schools of education, teachers in training take courses in pedagogy, lesson planning, mathematics, social studies, etc. Student teachers are routinely given instruction on the latest in teaching trends, but, in many cases, they are not required to demonstrate mastery of the subject they plan to teach. Elementary-level teachers receive instruction on how to teach reading, but they do not have to prove an ability to do so. Similarly, secondary-level teachers do not have to show an ability to teach the specific subject of their choice, such as math, English or science. As a consequence, teachers at any level who plan to teach in a specific subject area do not have to demonstrate academic mastery of that subject.

In 2006, Dr. Arthur Levine, former president of Teachers College, Columbia University, published a scathing report on our nation's schools of education.[72] Dr. Levine describes schools of education as, "programs that teach outdated curricula and failed to keep pace with demographics, technology, global competition and pressures to raise student achievement."[73] He also states that, "universities have exacerbated the situation by continuing to treat teacher-preparation programs as 'cash cows,' leading them to set low admission and graduation standards for their students."[74]

This latter point is particularly important, because most schools of education have, over time, become an important source of revenue to their host university. By setting low admission standards, they are catering to our least-qualified young people. In many universities, the program with the lowest average student SAT scores is the school of education. "One study found that college graduates whose SAT or ACT scores were in the bottom quartile were more than twice as likely as those in the top quartile to have majored in education."[75] Another study found that just 14 percent of college graduates with a major in education had SAT or ACT scores in the top quartile.[76]

However, our society clearly needs the best and brightest people to go into teaching, and that is not occurring. To change this situation, we must remove, or radically modify, our state certification laws. I'm not suggesting that we eliminate schools of education, but we must induce

---

72. Arthur Levine, *Educating School Teachers* (Washington, D.C.: Education Schools Project, 2006).
73. Ibid., 1.
74. Ibid., 4.
75. The Teaching Commission, "Teaching at Risk: A Call to Action" (2004), 17.
76. U.S. Department of Education, Office of Policy Planning and Innovation, "Meeting the Highly Qualified Teachers Challenge: The Secretary's Second Annual Report on Teacher Quality" (Washington, D.C.), 46.

them to prove their ability to train and graduate effective teachers. In eliminating their monopoly position, schools of education would have to do just that. The net effect would be the closure of some schools of education and the dramatic restructuring of others.

The idea of repealing state certification laws is not as radical as it may seem at first. Most faculty members at schools of education are themselves not certified. Nor are their peers in the other programs of a university. University professors are not required to be "certified" under state law. Nor are the faculty members of community colleges or private K–12 schools. The only education organization in our entire society that are restricted by law to hiring only teachers approved by an official school of education are our public schools. Another bizarre fact is that less than half of our schools of education, only 550 out of 1,400, are accredited (assuming for the moment that school accreditation has any more validity than teacher certification). This double weakness (uncertified professors in unaccredited schools) means many, perhaps most, teachers are certified by an educational process presented by uncertified staff in unaccredited institutions.[77]

Current certification laws focus on ensuring that new teachers spend a fixed number of hours studying at a school of education. The laws do not focus on professional competency, nor do they specify that new teachers show mastery of subject matter. Certification laws are very much like many graduation requirements; the focus is on student "seat time" rather than learning.

Today, in education schools, we try to teach students how to teach content, instead of training content-competent people how to teach. We have it backwards.

This has created the following situation in our country. Having highly qualified teachers for every class is especially problematic when

77. David W. Kirkpatrick, Alexis de Tocqueville Institution, "Teacher Certification Procedures are a Joke!" (June, 2000), 1, http://www.schoolreport.com/schoolreport/articles/certification_joke_6_00.htm.

the current science and mathematics teachers in the profession do not have science or mathematics backgrounds. Approximately 25 percent of high school mathematics teachers and 20 percent of high school science teachers don't have even a minor in their teaching field.

Because of the shortage of science and mathematics teachers, licensed teachers in other subject areas are often asked to teach science or mathematics. For 56 percent of high school students taking physical science classes and 27 percent of high school students taking mathematics classes, their teachers are teaching out of field. These percentages are higher in high-poverty schools."[78]

Students cannot learn from teachers who don't know their subject. This is especially true in math and science. "About two-thirds of the students studying chemistry and physics in U.S. high schools are taught by teachers with no major [degree] or certificate in the subject. In the case of math taught in grades five through twelve, the fraction is one-half. Many such students are being taught math by graduates in physical education."[79]

I am not the only one who believes that "certification" is not synonymous with effective teaching. A survey of superintendents and principals, done by Public Agenda, found that only 13 percent of principals and seven percent of superintendents believe that certification guarantees a typical teacher "has what it takes" to make it in the classroom.[80]

An article in the Society for Quality Education quoted a report by UCLA professor W. James Popham, who demonstrated on three separate occasions that teachers trained in teachers colleges do no better than laymen (housewives, automobile mechanics, and electricians) in

---

78. D. R. Sterling, "The Teacher Shortage: National Trends for Science and Mathematics," *Journal of Mathematics and Science* 7 (2004), 85–96. http://www.math.vcu.edu/g1/journal/Journal7/Part%20I/Sterling.html.

79. Norm R. Augustine, "Rising Above The Gathering Storm," Statement before the Committee on Science, U.S. House of Representatives (October 20, 2005).

80. Public Agenda, "An Assessment of Survey Data on Attitudes about Teaching, Including the Views of Parents, Administrators, Teachers and the General Public," compiled for The Teaching Commission, 20.

promoting student achievement: "The housewives, electricians and auto mechanics were exactly as effective as the professionally trained, credentialed, experienced teachers."[81] Teacher preparation as provided by colleges of education does not result in increased student achievement.

This is supported by teachers themselves when asked about the preparation they received in their school of education. "About 62 percent of all new teachers—almost two thirds—report they felt unprepared for the realities of their classroom. As Secretary of Education Arne Duncan has said, "Imagine what our country would do if 62 percent of our doctors felt unprepared to practice medicine—you would have a revolution in our medical schools."[82]

Is it any wonder our children do not do well academically? For a student to become mentally engaged in a subject, the student needs a teacher who is passionate about the subject and who can stimulate his or her intellectual interest and natural curiosity. Teachers without subject-matter mastery simply cannot do that; and we are now living with the results. Today, the United States has the lowest percentage of college students studying math or science of any country in the developed world.[83] As is well known, scientists and engineers are the fuel of any modern economy. If we are serious about STEM (science, technology, engineering and math) training for our young people, the only way to make that happen is to ensure we have content-competent teachers instructing our students.

However, the failure to teach our children math and science is not just about scientists and engineers; rather it is a major failing in the preparation of our children for any scholarly endeavor in which they may choose to engage. Basic skills in math and science are valuable for all

---

81. "The Loss of Our Faculties," *Society for Quality Education* (June 7, 2011), http://www.societyforqualityeducation.org/index.php/blog/the-loss-of-our-faculties.
82. "Teachers Want to Lead Their Profession's Transformation," *Education Week* (February 8, 2012), 24, http://www.edweek.org/ew/articles/2012/02/08/20debose.h31.html.
83. Robert Herbold, President's Council of Advisors on Science and Technology, "K–12 Establishment is Putting America's Industrial Leadership at Risk," speech on May 25, 2004, Seattle, Washington, http://www.freerepublic.com/focus/f-news/1341254/posts.

citizens to possess, regardless of the career or job they eventually choose. However, as discussed earlier, a well-educated child needs to learn much more than math or science.

Certification laws also discourage competent people from joining the teaching profession because they require everyone, including experienced professionals, to return to college for a teaching degree. That means people who already have had a successful career must become "certified" to do something they may already know how to do. Young people who earned a different degree in college (not in their college's school of education), such as math, biology or English, cannot work as a teacher in a public school without taking at least another year of college in an approved school of education. Older people, who have had a successful career in another profession, such as the sciences, journalism or the military, and would like to transfer into teaching find they have to return to college and get a formal teaching certificate. In some cases, that can require years of additional college and tuition expenses, all to teach a subject a career professional may have already mastered.

For example, no symphony conductor would be allowed to teach music. Bill Gates, without a formal teaching certificate, would not be allowed to teach computer science, no retired astronaut would be allowed to teach math or astronomy. No veteran would be allowed to teach physical education, or a course in leadership. These are extreme examples perhaps, but they are genuinely illustrative. Throughout the country there are thousands of highly qualified people who would like to teach, perhaps because they would like an exciting change of work, or because they like the idea of helping young people, but they are prevented from doing so because they are not formally "certified."

One evening I was having dinner with a woman who had spent 15 years in the advertising business. She had earned a bachelor's degree and a master of business administration degree, and her position at the time was CEO of an advertising firm. She had done very well in her career and had decided she would like to have a second career. She wanted to become a teacher. She visited one of her state's schools of education and was told she would have to enter as a freshman in order to get her teaching certificate. She decided to stay in advertising—a clear loss for students and for our public schools.

Recent experience with many Teach For America teachers has shown that non-certified instructors can do exemplary work in the classroom. Many of these young graduates, from some of our finest colleges, have achieved amazing results, even with the hardest-to-teach kids. These young people, who evince a passion for teaching, are producing some of the greatest academic gains in some of our lowest-performing schools. They are proving that even children living in the most destitute home conditions can perform at exemplary levels when provided with focused, quality instruction. The Teach For America program shows that the problem with our public schools has little to do with our children's supposed inability to learn, but everything to do with our adults' real ability to teach.

Finding qualified people willing to teach is not the problem, as demonstrated by the experience of The New Teacher Project (TNTP). TNTP is a nonprofit organization that recruits skilled people into the teaching profession. In 2006, TNTP was asked to hire 1,200 teachers to staff low-performing schools for the New York City Public Schools. It received over 8,000 applications. Some the applicants were doctors, lawyers, business people and researchers. None of the applicants were formally certified under New York State's normal process, but the 1,200 people selected were put through a teacher-training program, managed by the TNTP, and then placed in a public school. Each new teacher was assigned a mentor to assist during the first year of teaching. Regardless of the city in whichTNTP is seeking recruits, it receives many more applicants than open positions.

Moreover, because of the large applicant pool, TNTP is able to be selective and TNTP leaders can ensure that only highly qualified people enter the classroom. Frankly, this is how the entire process of public school hiring should be managed.

Of course, not every school of education is a poor one. I have visited many excellent schools and have become friends with their deans. However, I am talking about a few excellent schools of education, not hundreds. Based upon Dr. Levine's assessment, the vast majority of schools charged with granting teaching certificates are not good at their task and have no business preparing professionals to teach our children. These mediocre schools exist to collect tuition and to turn out people with a teaching credential. They do not exist to train teachers who are effective educators. The measure of teacher effectiveness should be the ability to improve student learning (outcomes) and not the number of courses completed at a school of education (inputs).

Schools of education have not shown they can turn out great teachers, and state certification laws have not provided a reliable supply of qualified teachers in the classroom. Both systems need to be changed.

We should either eliminate the notion of certification or modify it dramatically so that teacher certification is something one earns, on the job, after proving that children actually learn effectively under one's instruction. If we must maintain the state requirement of certification, then I recommend that we modify the laws to require a minimum of three years of in-class teaching before one qualifies for certification.

I believe, however, that certification laws should simply be eliminated, and that schools of education should justify their existence by proving that completing their training programs significantly enhances a teacher's ability. Business schools operate exactly this way, and it works.

Ending certification restrictions would yield other benefits as well. First, many poor-quality education schools would close, and those that remained would be in greater demand because they would be able to demonstrate that their course work is beneficial to making their graduates good teachers. Having fewer and better schools of education would make entry into the profession more competitive. One of the fastest ways to enhance the profession of teaching would be to make it more difficult to enter.

Schools and districts need to raise teaching standards, and in response schools of education need to raise their admission requirements. Eliminating certification laws is the first step to enhancing educational training and to building up the stature of the teaching profession.

An example of this occurred in Finland. Back in the 1980s, the Finnish government determined that, "education was the only thing that could save their country from being left behind," reported Amanda Ripley in *The Smartest Kids in the World*.

The Finns decided that the only way to get serious about education was to select highly educated people, the best and brightest of each generation, and train them rigorously. So, that's what they did."[84] Today, Finland has the highest-performing students in the world and the result is a transformed country.

One of the steps the Finns took was to dismantle their existing education schools. Like the U.S. does today, Finland had many small education colleges around the country. Today, it has only a few located in major universities. Entry into one of these schools is as difficult as getting into a medical school. Only about 10 percent of those who apply are able to get in. Teaching has become a very "high status" profession in Finland.

A 2010 study by McKinsey and Company found that 100 percent of new teachers in the best-performing school systems in the world—Finland, Singapore and South Korea—come from the top third of their college classes. In contrast, 77 percent of new U.S. teachers come from the bottom two-thirds of their college classes.[85]

---

84. Amanda Ripley, *The Smartest Kids in the World* (New York: Simon and Schuster, 2013), 89.
85. Byron Auguste, Paul Kinn and Matt Miller, "Closing the talent gap: Attacting and retaining top third graduates to a career in teaching," McKinsey & Co. (September 2010), 1, http://mckinseyonsociety.com/closing-the-talent-gap/.

By having only their brightest people entering the profession, the Finns were able to deregulate their schools and give both principals and teachers total freedom on how they taught their students. They were able to, "dismantle its most oppressive regulations, piece by piece.... The government abolished school inspections. It didn't need them anymore"[86] As the Finns deregulated their schools they enhanced the profession of teaching by giving teachers and principals the kind of autonomy that other professionals enjoy.

Also, by reducing the number of education schools and restricting admission, they made education schools become more relevant in the preparation of teachers. Attending one of these schools became a requirement, not because of certification laws, but because they turned out proven teachers.

Another outcome of certification laws, combined with tenure, is that teaching has become a career occupation. This situation results in our children having teachers who have usually spent their entire working lives in the classroom. In some cases that may be desirable, but often these teachers then cannot impart many of life's skills that one acquires from having other life experiences. As was pointed out earlier, the mission of a school involves the "total development" of a child. That includes much more than academics. Restricting the profession to teachers who have never had another job, who have never engaged in any other life endeavor, greatly limits their scope of teaching. Typically, the most-remembered and best college professors were those with experiences outside of the classroom, who could bring real life experiences into their daily lessons. We need to bring the same benefit to our public schools. Today, because of certification laws, very little discussion of wider life experiences occurs in the classroom.

Removing certification laws would also allow tens of thousands of citizens, who have developed skills and wonderful experiences, and who would love to teach children, to get into the profession. Former members

---

86. Amanda Ripley, *The Smartest Kids*, 89.

of the military, mid-career professionals and retirees from government, nonprofits or business are examples. We do our children a great disservice by preventing these citizens from doing so.

Certification laws are the "gatekeeper" of education, and these laws are keeping the most qualified people out of the profession. Eliminating, or substantially modifying, certification laws is the fastest way to correct all of these teaching-quality problems and to enhance the stature of the teaching profession.

2. Placement and Working Conditions

HIRING OF new teachers normally occurs in the summer and a new teacher begins teaching in the fall. In the few weeks (sometimes only days) between being hired and the start of the school year, a new teacher is expected to prepare for students. Seldom will a new teacher be given a mentor or extensive teaching materials such as lesson plans, or provided with useful information from the prior teacher who taught in that classroom. Also, a teacher is generally given minimal, if any, information about the learning readiness of her students. Thus, in many cases, a new teacher must "reinvent the wheel" when embarking upon his or her teaching career.

If all these conditions weren't difficult enough, early on-the-job training is often nonexistent, unlike other professions. A new teacher is expected to know at the outset what to do, and how to do it. Some do, and some don't. New teachers are generally given the most difficult students to teach in the most resource-poor schools. This occurs because experienced teachers use seniority to choose both the schools where they work and the students they will teach. In no other profession would the newest hires be given the most difficult assignments. Such mismatched work assignments would not even be considered, let alone tolerated, in other fields.

Some new teachers are lucky to begin work at a school with an outstanding principal. When that occurs, new teachers have someone to help them adjust to new surroundings and to offer assistance. When that help is not there, and often it is not, new teachers are still expected to perform at a high level.

Unlike other professions, the "best practices" learned in teaching are seldom shared, even within a school building, let alone across a whole district. The reason is that all teachers are scheduled to be in class with students at the same time, which hinders a new teacher from observing or being mentored by an experienced educator.

Working conditions in many schools are also appalling. In some cases the buildings are old and poorly maintained: bathrooms don't always work, paint is chipping off walls, hallways are cluttered, graffiti remains on the walls, etc. In many cases, there aren't enough textbooks or supplies. I could go on, but, sufice to say, some of our teachers face many other problems than just poorly prepared students.

Teachers just entering the profession need to be treated the way starting doctors and engineers are treated. They need to work initially with experts to hone their skills. A doctor does not come out of medical school ready to perform major surgery. That skill is learned over several years while being guided by a skilled surgeon. The same is true for engineers. A new engineer is considered an apprentice until passing a licensing exam and obtaining a good deal of on-the-job training under the tutelage of an experienced engineer. In no case is a newly trained doctor or engineer given the most difficult patient or project right from the start.

Another aspect of teaching that restricts a teacher's ability to succeed is the regimented school day and the lack of time teachers have to prepare for their students.

Betty Wallace and William Graves described a teacher's life in *The Poisoned Apple*.

> Anyone who has taught in public schools will understand why teachers rely on textbooks. They are daily expected to deliver at least five, sometimes more, forty-five minute lessons. Typically, they have at most one period a day to prepare. It is as impossible for a teacher to

prepare five interesting presentations a day, as it would be for a pastor to prepare five daily sermons or for a politician to develop a new speech for every campaign stop.[87]

When we informed the Chinese teachers that American elementary school teachers are responsible for their classes all day long, they looked incredulous. How could any teacher be expected to do a good job when there is not time outside of class to prepare and correct lessons, work with individual children, consult with other teachers and attend to all the matters that arise in a typical day at school?[88]

Focus group discussions with teachers all over the country have shown that job satisfaction is the biggest problem facing teachers. Surveys measuring job satisfaction show that lack of support and not being treated with respect rank above compensation in importance.[89] This is not surprising since those entering the profession know, in advance, what their compensation will be. It is also not surprising that teachers constantly push to receive more money, because they do not have control over other factors that impact respect and job satisfaction. If you don't like your working conditions, it is normal to complain that you do not make enough money.

If teachers could enter the profession with ongoing support to help them be successful in the classroom, many young teachers would remain in the profession, even with the compensation they now receive. Frustration with their inability to be successful, that is, to see that children learn under their tutelage, drives many teachers to pursue other vocations. Fixing this aspect of the teaching profession would dramatically reduce turnover, would improve student achievement and would greatly increase teacher job satisfaction, even if we didn't significantly boost compensation.

---

87. Betty Wallace and William Graves, *The Poisoned Apple* (New York: St. Martin's Press, 1995), 37.
88. William Stevenson and James W. Stigler, *The Learning Gap* (New York: Summit Books, 1992), 175.
89. "Lessons Learned" *Public Agenda* 1 (2007), 25, http://www.publicagenda.org/files/lessons_learned_1.pdf.

3. Compensation

Teachers' compensation comes in two types, base compensation, which is the pay that all teachers receive, and incentitive compensation, which results from additional training or on-job performance.

Base Compensation

Almost everyone, including legislators, agrees that teachers do not make enough money. Teaching is a skilled occupation and yet many people in the profession can hardly afford to pay the rent. Teachers working in urban and affluent suburban school systems claim they often cannot afford to live in the district where they work. Many in the profession believe they are over-worked, under-appreciated and underpaid.

Most teachers will tell you they work many more hours than the length of the workday for which they are paid. Good teachers will spend two to three hours a night correcting papers and preparing for the next day's classes. Moreover, teachers attend classes during the summer and on school days arrive early to get ready for students. None of this time is compensated. This, of course, is not unique to teaching. Most professions have people who often work evenings and weekends, if needed, without additional compensation.

In almost all states, teacher pay is driven by a salary schedule depending on years of service and academic credits obtained. Nothing in the compensation system rewards teaching excellence. This type of structured compensation system was installed in the 1920s "to ensure equal treatment for all."[90]

Over the intervening ninety years our entire society has changed, but the compensation system for teachers has remained the same, except that the dollar amounts in the schedule have dramatically increased. The current compensation system rewards mediocrity at the same rate as excellence. No other profession operates this way.

---

90. Allan Odden, "Rewarding Expertise," *Education Next* 1, no. 1 (Spring 2001), http://educationnext.org/rewarding-expertise/.

The current teacher compensation system is broken and needs to be totally changed. I would argue, however, that compensation changes are needed more to make teaching a true profession than to dramatically improve the quality of people who enter it.

Though teachers do not earn as much money as people in some other professions, if you look carefully, you will find the problem is not a matter of compensation at all. It is a matter of employment. **Teachers are not underpaid or underworked, they are underemployed.**

That is perhaps a radical statement, but the hourly compensation of teachers is really quite competitive with other professions. The average teacher in most states is paid a very attractive hourly wage. For example, Average teacher pay in Seattle is $70,850 for a ten-month work year.[91] That is low for the annual compensation of a trained professional. However, that same teacher is actually making $53.67 an hour, plus a generous package of benefits that few private-sector employers can match. Teachers in Seattle are employed for 1,320 hours per year, regardless of how many hours they might actually work. If that teacher were employed for a standard year of 2,080 hours, at the same hourly rate, their annual salary would be $111,642, a very competitive salary for a college graduate. Bear in mind, this comparison is based on the average salary. Thus, some teachers are making substantially more than that amount, while new teachers make less.

The above numbers are based upon an urban system (Seattle). Some states are paying more than that and some less. The highest average pay for a teacher is in the state of New York, where teachers average $75,279 statewide.[92] South Dakota has the lowest average compensation at $39,580.[93] Those differences reflect the substantial difference in cost of

---

91. The above numbers are based upon Seattle, but they are comparable for urban districts across the country. Liv Finne, "Key Facts about Seattle Public Schools," Washington Policy Center, (January 2011), http://www.washingtonpolicy.org/publications/facts/key-facts-about-seattle-public-schools.
92. National Center for Education Statistics, *Digest of Education Statistics*, 2013, Table 211.60.
93. Ibid.

living between those two states. Using the same 2080 hour year, these equate to $118,615 and $62,370, respectively, plus a benefit package that is well above that found in major corporations.

Looking at the above analysis, it becomes obvious that what we have is an employment problem, not a compensation problem. The way for teachers to make more money is to employ them for more hours in the year. One quick move would be to employ teachers for eight hours a day. Today, a Seattle elementary teacher is employed for seven hours a day and a secondary teacher for seven-and-a-half hours a day. Just employing them for the standard eight hours would generate a seven to fourteen percent increase in compensation, and would begin to close the gap between the hours compensated and the actual number of hours worked. It would also allow principals more time with teachers for staff meetings, evaluation meetings, student assessment and curriculum planning. Additionally, it would allow teachers more time to spend with students and other teachers during and after the school day.

Further, it is obvious that as our schools move to create standards-based learning environments, some children will need to attend class for more hours per day and more days per year in order to achieve the academic standard. Not all children can and do learn the same amount of information in the same amount of time. This means that, to ensure the education of all children, schools will need to stay open longer, and that means some teachers will be employed for more hours. See Chapter 9 for more information on this issue.

This evolving situation presents both a requirement and an opportunity. Currently, all teachers are employed for the 180-day school year, even though they are paid a fixed amount per month. Erroneously, teacher compensation is often considered as an annual salary when, in reality, it is a nine month salary. In fact, it is even less than a nine-month salary because teachers are employed only seven hours per day and school is not in session every work day during those nine months.

It is obvious, however, that some people go into teaching because they like having summers off and because it allows them to be home when their children are home. This is not something that is likely to change, nor need it change for all teachers.

Recognizing that fact suggests we should think about hiring teachers under different annual contracts. For example, teachers could choose to work for nine months, ten months or eleven months. Those choosing the ten or eleven month contracts would make substantially more money, but they obviously wouldn't get summers off. Those teachers could work with students who need more learning time before moving to the next level, or as mentors for new teachers before the start of a new school year. Teachers would indicate their desired contract year, and district officials would decide which teachers to hire under each type of contract.

Incentive Compensation

Longer contracts would create a way for teachers to receive a professional level of compensation, but longer contracts would not solve the problem of incentive. Even under longer contracts, mediocre teachers could receive as much or more money than excellent teachers.

The current system allows a teacher to make more money only by accumulating seniority or earning more credits and degrees from a school of education. Neither criterion gives any indication of whether the teacher has improved his or her instructional skill or is more effective in helping children learn. Thus, a very poor teacher with 20 years of experience will earn more than an excellent teacher with five years of experience. No other profession works this way.

To rectify this, I recommend the establishment of "career ladders" for the profession. This would allow excellence to be rewarded by making a promotion ladder available to teachers who excel.

Teachers should be paid based on their ability, not on their years of service. Teaching talent can be measured by the learning that occurs in the classroom. Teachers whose students learn under their tutelage should make more money than teachers who fail to educate children effectively. In fact, an ineffective teacher should not be allowed to remain in the classroom, wasting students' learning time.

With a career ladder, a good teacher has access to a future of increasing compensation based on performance. A career ladder would include job titles corresponding to levels such as Apprentice Teacher, Teacher, Senior Teacher and Master Teacher. A teacher would be promoted to the next level only after a certain number of years and a series of positive evaluations. Such a program would reward performance, and would give teachers the opportunity to increase their income while remaining in the profession. Teachers who did not get promoted beyond an apprentice level after a few years would be invited to leave the profession.

You will note that I have not recommended any incentive compensation program. Though many people promote the notion of merit pay, I have come to the conclusion that it is not a good idea. Merit pay does not always provide the intended outcomes, and could obstruct the faculty from operating like a high-performance work team.

I once studied the functioning of a school district that had implemented merit pay. The outcome was not what had been intended. Teachers who received the merit pay were unwilling to share their teaching expertise for fear of not getting a merit bonus the following year (there was a limited amount of bonus funds available). Teachers who failed to get merit pay tended to ostracize those who did. Both responses were detrimental to the academic effectiveness of a school.

Another reason individual merit pay is not practical in public schools is that each teacher is very dependent on the teacher who taught the students in the prior year. For example, the 'internal customer' of a first-grade teacher is the second-grade teacher. If the first-grade teacher fails to prepare the students, then the second-grade teacher's ability to advance student learning will suffer, even if the second-grade teacher is truly outstanding. All members of the faculty must carry their weight if all students are to achieve. If one teacher fails to do the job properly, the next teacher in line is hindered in his or her work. Each teacher must strive to deliver to the next teacher students who have achieved their learning goals for that grade level. This is the primary reason why merit pay does not work.

If we want to incentivize teachers beyond the career ladder mentioned above, then I would favor "whole school" bonuses rather than individual merit pay. Providing a bonus opportunity for the entire faculty would give every teacher a strong financial incentive and provide built-in pressure for every teacher to perform.

Conclusion

IF WE are serious about educating all of our children, we must alter the ways we select, train and compensate our teachers. Improving the selection and training of teachers would not cost extra money; in fact it may well be done with less money, with substantially improved results. The ideas presented here that involve compensation will require more money. However, every state is already spending a lot of money in dealing with high turnover and having to hire and train new teachers to replace those who leave the profession. Those costs are never accounted for, but they are substantial, not only in dollars, but in reduced student achievement.

Providing students with access to gifted teachers during a longer day and a longer year would create a good chance of keeping those kids in school through graduation, ready to secure good jobs or more education. This would reduce the costs we now spend on the juvenile justice system and on the social services provided by the federal and state governments. Universities and community colleges would also save money by not having to provide extensive remedial courses. Further, better-educated students would yield increased tax revenues, as these students graduate and become productive, tax- paying citizens.

With the exception of eliminating certification laws, none of these ideas need be implemented immediately. They could be phased in over several years. Increasing the number of hours teachers are employed could grow as gradually as the state could afford. Every hour added would make the profession more attractive and would reduce turnover. Adding experienced mentors would also be a great addition to improving teacher job satisfaction.

Today, there are thousands of wonderfully qualified people in the teaching profession. They remain in the profession in spite of the obstacles described in this chapter. We owe it to them, and to those who will follow, to treat them and compensate them like the professionals they are. Teaching is perhaps our most vital profession, but we are not devoting the time or money required to make the profession all it needs to be. By not doing so, we have discouraged our best and brightest people from entering the teaching profession and we have deprived our children of the teachers they both need and deserve.

6.

LEADERSHIP

WHY IS IT SOME SCHOOLS PROPEL EVERY CHILD TO REACH HIGH achievement levels and others do not—sometimes even among schools in the same district? Why is it some schools have very few disruptions by students and others, with similar student populations, have constant discipline problems? Why is it some schools have virtually no staff turnover and others have a revolving door of staff? Why is it some schools have very high student and staff attendance rates and other schools do not? The answer to each of these questions rests with the quality of leadership present in the building.

High-performing schools share many characteristics, but none is more important than leadership. **A visionary principal always leads an effective school.** In fact, it is impossible for a school to become effective without the leadership of a visionary leader who is able to rally the support and commitment of the entire faculty and parent community, regardless of the makeup of the student body. The same is true for a school district.

Some people who are frustrated with the quality of public education believe it can be improved only by the use of charters, vouchers, or both. However, even at a charter school or under a voucher system, effective leadership is the primary driver of success.

As with any organization, the impact of effective leadership on a school's performance is profound. A recent study by Branch, Hanushek and Rivkin found that, "a highly effective principal raises student achievement by from two to seven additional months of learning in a single school year."[94] A study in 2004, funded by the Wallace Foundation, found that 25 percent of student achievement can be traced to the school leader.[95] Can you imagine what our schools would be like if they were all led by effective principals?

Unfortunately, public education is virtually devoid of effective leadership. I say this knowing full well that we have some absolutely amazing schools operating inside public education. However, those schools number in the hundreds, at best a thousand or so, among almost 100,000 schools nationwide. We also do not have a single major district that can be considered highly effective in educating all students. If we had effective leadership throughout the system, that would not be the case.

So why is public education nearly devoid of effective leaders? We addressed this issue in Chapter 1, by pointing out that the present system promotes educators based not upon who has proven leadership ability, but upon who wants to be an education administrator. Leadership development in public education is a process-driven system, not a competency-driven system. Further, the quality of any leadership training provided is sorely lacking.

Richard Elmore, a professor of educational leadership at Harvard, says it this way:

> the vast majority of people who are certified as educational leaders still come from largely part-time, cash-for-credit certification programs in small institutions, operating under traditional state-certification requirements, without significant research capacity, and staffed heavily by part-time faculty members.[96]

---

94. Gregory F. Branch, Eric A. Hanushek and Steven G. Rivkin, "School Leaders Matter," *Education Next* 13, no. 1 (Winter 2013), http://educationnext.org/school-leaders-matter/.

95. "How Leadership Improves Student Learning" *Wallace Foundation* (September 2004), 5.

96. Richard Elmore, *School Reform from the Inside Out: Policies, Practices and Performance* (Cambridge, Mass: Harvard Education Press, 2004), 59.

Moreover, in most states, there are numerous institutions licensed to grant teacher and principal certificates. A person could be a terrible teacher and still be accepted into one of these principal training programs. Acceptance virtually assures graduation, and graduation virtually ensures employment, because we have a shortage of principals. Further, once hired, one is virtually assured of gaining tenure. Each step leads invariably to the next, and tenure provides functional lifetime employment for even the most incompetent leaders. Elmore goes on to say:

> And despite the existence of the ISLC (Interstate School Leaders Licensure Consortium) standards, empirical evidence on the state of curriculum and teaching in leadership-preparation programs paints a picture of relatively low-level content that is disconnected from mainstream research and practice in public and private organizations outside the education sector. The existence of alternative programs and providers has not broken the traditional cartel of higher education institutions, state departments of education, and local districts that has controlled leadership preparation for a century or more.[97]

This method of training, hiring and promoting leaders is unique to public education, which is the only professional segment of our society in which **promotion is based on self-selection**. Almost any teacher can decide to become a principal, and, once the decision has been made, can become one. All a teacher has to do is leave the classroom for a year and attend an education college for the required courses to obtain a principal certification. In fact, it has been shown that our worst teachers are often the first to apply to become principals. A common refrain is that 'if you can't make it in the classroom, go into administration.'

As was pointed out earlier, this same procedure is followed for choosing superintendents. In most states, superintendents must also be certified. The state's education colleges also grant this credential. Education training programs, particularly for superintendents, are faulty in both their entry requirements and their curricula. Many of the skills required be a good superintendent, particularly for an urban school district, are

---

97. Ibid., 60.

not taught in schools of education. Consequently, most superintendents come out of these programs poorly equipped for the job and, in most cases, lacking in leadership talent as well.

The whole system of promotion and leadership development in public education is broken. The most effective principals and superintendents report they became effective leaders "in spite of the system, not because of it."

As was the case for teachers, the source of this problem is certification laws. These laws again give a monopoly to education schools for the development of education leaders. Frankly, the last place on any college campus that I would look for leaders would be the education school, but that is the only place our schools can look. Unless and until we change this, our education system will continue to be devoid of effective leadership.

Strong leaders will enable improvements for the system as a whole, regardless of any lesser decisions a government or school district makes. Effective educational leaders will not tolerate the system we have now; they would find a way to change it, one way or another.

Two examples of this point can be seen in the actions of Rod Paige, former superintendent of Houston Public Schools who later became the U.S. secretary of education, and John Stanford, the former major general who became superintendent of Seattle Public Schools. Both men were leaders; one was a formally trained educator and one was not.

Rod Paige was a teacher, a football coach, a college professor and then dean of a school of education before becoming superintendent of the Houston Public Schools. His background training and innate talents made him an effective education leader. During his tenure, Houston made great strides in decentralizing decision-making and in improving academic achievement for all students. Paige's leadership skills were developed over time, as he took on new and increasingly challenging positions. By the time he became a superintendent, he not only had the skills needed for the job, but he had the knowledge of what was needed to fix a major urban public education system. Houston, under Paige's leadership, was touted nationally as one of the premier examples of an urban school district on the mend.

John Stanford served thirty years in the U.S. Army. He once told me that ten of those thirty years were spent in some type of training. Stanford attended Pennsylvania State University for his bachelor's degree and received a master's degree in public policy from Michigan State University. He also attended the Army War College and completed numerous leadership-training courses during his time in the Army. Throughout his military career, he held a variety of leadership positions, including leading troops in combat. Upon retiring from the military, General Stanford was appointed county executive of Fulton County, Georgia (the county that includes Atlanta). In less than four years General Stanford was able to completely restructure county government, install over $1 billion of infrastructure improvements, put the county's financial house in order and do it all without raising taxes.

By the time General Stanford became superintendent of Seattle Public Schools, he had honed his leadership skills to a very fine level. In his two-and-a-half years as superintendent not only did he transform Seattle Public Schools, but he transformed the attitude of an entire city toward its public school system, achieving widespread support. He eliminated mandatory busing, decentralized decision-making, installed a new funding policy and negotiated a union contract that eliminated seniority in the hiring of teachers. He became gravely ill during the last six months of his tenure and, sadly, died of leukemia 38 months after becoming superintendent.

Both individuals, and their accomplishments, are classic examples of the power of effective leadership. Effective leaders can create a movement, even in an entrenched bureaucracy. However, that is unlikely to happen in our education system, as we have so few effective leaders and the current leadership training system is unlikely to change that. In addition, those leaders outside the system who would like to bring their skills to education are unable to do so because they cannot get in. One way to develop effective leadership is to overhaul the method of promotion.

Businesses and the military have promotion processes in place that the education community could emulate. In the business world, promotion occurs on the basis of evaluation and proven performance. Generally, when a person is promoted, he or she is given additional training either inside or outside the company, but in either case paid for by the company. Sometimes, companies will even send outstanding employees back to college. Many companies will gladly pay for some or all of the cost of a master of business administration (MBA) program for their most valued employees. Large companies such as General Electric, IBM, Microsoft, and Motorola have their own advanced training centers for employees, where they invest heavily in cultivating leaders for a future role in their respective organizations.

MBA programs at most universities have stringent entrance requirements. Only the best and brightest are admitted. Typically, they have already distinguished themselves in some field and have survived a rigorous screening process. Thus, MBA applicants have already demonstrated leadership talent before they enter the program. Graduates of these programs either return to their employer, if the employer sent them to school or contributed to tuition, or or they obtain a junior-level management position with a company. In both cases, an individual is not promoted until he or she has proven an ability to perform in a leadership position.

The military operates in a similar way. Promotions are based upon performance evaluations. Additionally, many officers graduate from a military academy that has very competitive entrance requirements and that admits only the most outstanding applicants. Graduates leave the academies as second lieutenants or ensigns and start up the ladder of promotion based upon performance.

If public education selected, trained and promoted talented employees in this fashion, schools would quickly improve, because only the best candidates would become principals. Thus, only those properly prepared would be placed in a leadership position. The same would be true of superintendents.

Public education is a government activity, so proposed changes may correlate better from the military illustration rather than from business. For example, the federal government fully funds four major universities (the military academies) for the sole purpose of training leaders for our military. These four institutions provide each branch of the military with a constant supply of well-trained, carefully selected leaders who have the capacity to maintain our country's military readiness and defend our nation.

There is no similar leadership training for public education. There is not even one institution, fully funded by the federal, state, or local governments established to train leaders for our schools. It is time we founded a West Point for education—though I would suggest a two-year school, rather than West Point's four-year undergraduate model. The graduate school would operate much like advanced business schools and be funded like the military academies. Such an institution or institutions would accept only outstanding candidates who were certain of their desire to be an educational leader, passed a rigorous application process and showed meaningful leadership skills in their early professional work. Educators graduating from such a school, or schools, would receive a master of education administration (MEA) and would be hired as vice principals in large schools, or perhaps directly as principals in small schools.

Fully funded by the government, these schools could be separate institutions, or simply be leadership academies created on college campuses. Students would accept government-funded tuition and board in exchange for a four-year commitment to the field of public education. If the education-leadership academy was integrated into a university program, then the government funding could funnel to students differently, such as through scholarship awards, with the same four-year commitment to the field of public education required.

If the federal government was unwilling to set up such institutions, then states could act. In fact, we need multiple schools for this purpose, so it might be more practical and make more sense to have states take on this assignment. As I indicated, these schools could become part of an existing state university.

Such a school or schools would offer an interdisciplinary curriculum, including courses in subjects relevant to the job of principal and superintendent. Professors from education, business, public policy and even medicine would be employed. Students would be exposed to problems likely to be faced by an education leader. Issues such as employee evaluations, hiring skills, labor relations, finance and budgeting, public relations and media, and influencing politicians, would all be covered, in addition to basic courses in curriculum planning and effective teaching. Graduates would be well prepared and capable of becoming agents of change in their new positions. Would-be superintendents would also get training in construction management, bonding, marketing bonds and levies, union negotiations, etc.

An example of one such program was recently established at the University of Virginia. For the 2013–14 school year, the faculty of the Darden School (business) and the faculty of the Curry School (education) have developed a unique dual MBA/MEd. degree. Students begin at Curry during the first summer and then take traditional business courses at the Darden School during their first year. In their second summer, students take courses at Curry and can participate in an internship. In their second year, students take courses in both schools. Students admitted to this program have gone through the same admission process required of traditional Darden students.

Though it was assumed that the students entering the program would be interested in becoming education leaders such as principals and superintendents, the reality is that some students have even broader interests. Some want to go into consulting with a special focus on education while others want to start new charter schools or found education technology startups. Some are even interested in finance jobs that involve providing capital for new ventures or investing in public-for-profit companies that serve education.

Regardless of where these graduates end up, the program will turn out well-trained leaders with a passion for education. That can only be good for our schools. It will be interesting to see whether this program can achieve its lofty goals and whether it will be replicated elsewhere.

In addition to the creation of one or more national education academies, we must also develop programs to enhance the skills of current superintendents and principals. Such programs would be similar to the executive management programs offered by many business schools. These would be one- to six-week residential programs in which superintendents and principals would take courses designed to enhance their skills for their respective administrative positions. School districts and charitable foundations, along with state and federal governments would fund these programs. Most major universities could create these short-term intensive focused programs in concert with their education and business schools.

After discussing this idea in 2001 with then-Dean Kim Clark of the Harvard Business School (HBS), I was pleased to see that school engaged in furthering this exact model. HBS has partnered with the Harvard Graduate School of Education (HGSE) and has developed a program for superintendents and their immediate staff. The program is called the Public Education Leadership Project (PELP). The program started in 2003 and so far 29 school districts have participated in PELP with positive results. Arne Duncan, the current U.S. secretary of education, is a graduate of PELP. HBS has also published a book written by HBS and HGSE faculty covering case studies of various school districts and the issues they face. Over 45,000 copies have been sold and are now being used throughout the country.

The University of Virginia started a similar executive-management program composed of faculty members from the Darden School of Business and the Curry School of Education. Whereas the Harvard program trains superintendents and a school district's top seven managers, the Virginia program started by offering advanced training for 40 education leaders from two districts in Florida. Those 40 people included the superintendents and some management personnel, plus members of the community. Both programs started in 2003 and have received rave reviews from attendees. Since starting this effort, the Curry and Darden schools have worked with 75 districts from 15 states on improving district operations and on teaching principals and district leaders how to work together to turn around failing schools.

Charter schools are also working on leadership development. Their program is much more aligned with what is done in industry. Teachers, who are already carefully selected, are constantly assessed for their leadership skills and their willingness to take on leadership roles. Selected teachers are then given leadership assignments within their building. Assuming they perform those assignments satisfactorily, they are then selected to go into a principal-training program that will include extensive internships in schools led by outstanding principals. Upon graduation, they are given vice principal assignments. All schools have at least one vice principal, and in all of them the job of principal includes being a mentor to aspiring principals. Both the Knowledge Is Power Program (KIPP) and Summit Charter schools have programs similar to this. In both cases, they have decided to "grow their own," as they seldom can find acceptable candidates within the public system.

Conclusion

AMERICA'S PUBLIC education system needs to be transformed. Educational success for children will require superb leadership at all levels. Developing a system of selecting and training effective leaders is a necessary step to achieving that success. Such a system must be a top priority of federal and state education policy.

To begin this process, states need to eliminate certification laws. These laws have failed in their purpose and are now a major constraint to improving our schools. Without these laws, education schools would have to improve to retain their existence and other schools on a university campus could be employed in preparing both our teachers and our leaders for a future in education. In addition, without these laws, more people like John Stanford could be recruited into our education system, to the benefit of all our children.

Principal and superintendent training academies should be established in several locations around the country. These academies should be multidisciplinary institutions that set high and rigid standards for admission and for graduation, and turn out truly gifted leaders who have a passion for education.

The Harvard Business School accepts about 900 students per year, which means in ten years almost 9,000 people will have graduated with advanced business training. There are slightly more than 14,000 school districts in this country. However, half of America's children attend school in just 800 districts. If, ten years from now, schools and districts had even a few thousand well-trained leaders, we would have an entirely new educational system in this country.

Improving our schools is dependent upon improving the leadership in those schools. To make that happen, we must dramatically change the way we select and train education leaders.

7.

GOVERNANCE

LEADERSHIP FOR ANY ORGANIZATION STARTS AT THE TOP, AND FOR public school districts that means the school board. In most cases, the citizens of a community elect school board members, just as they do for a local mayor and city council members. Local control has been a core principle in public education governance since the inception of the common school. Locally elected school boards are perceived to be a key element to that control.

There are 13,588 school districts in the United States, and a school board leads each district.[98] The number of districts, and therefore the number of school boards, in a state varies considerably, ranging from 17 in Nevada to 1,043 in Texas. My state of Washington has 296 school districts. Boards vary in size, but most have five members. Large urban systems or county-wide districts will often have seven to nine members. Districts vary in size from the smallest, with a few hundred students to New York City, our country's largest district, with over 1,000,000 students.

The length of a school board term is normally four years. To ensure continuity, the terms are sequenced so a majority of school board member terms usually expire one year, and then the remaining board member terms expire two years later. This cycle of elections can cause a school board's entire membership to change in only four years.

---

98. National Center for Education Statistics, *Digest of Education Statistics*, 2012 Tables and Figures, Table 98.

Two or more candidates may run for each school board position. Thus, there are a lot of people running for office across each state, proposing a lot of different education agendas.

For most of the past century, board positions were filled by competent, caring people who ran for the school board as part of their civic duty. With small school systems and highly qualified people on the board, there existed strong governance. Today, that strong governance model still works well in some suburban and rural public school systems. However, in urban systems and even some larger suburban school districts, that is no longer the case. Some 800 districts have student populations in excess of 10,000, and these districts enroll slightly more than half of the nation's 50 million students.[99]

Being a board member of one of these larger districts is a much different job than being a board member in a small, rural district. In the larger districts, there can be hundreds of schools and dozens of neighborhoods involved. Candidates are not necessarily from the local neighborhood and are not necessarily a good fit for the office they seek. Candidates for school board are often poorly qualified, and sometimes their service is very detrimental to the effective management of the school system they oversee.

Often they do not understand the level of authority they have. School boards are policy-making bodies, not legislative or operational bodies. Thus, there is a limited number of areas in which boards should be involved. However, many board members do not understand their policy-making function, or they choose to ignore it and then interfere with management and district operations. They become log rollers for petty interests. Again, far from helping, a school board made up of such members can be actively detrimental to the effective operation of a school district.

---

99. David Kirkpatrick, "The Superintendency: Neither Inevitable nor Necessary," *Free Republic*, http://www.freerepublic.com/focus/f-news/1325624/posts.

The decline in the quality and competency of school board candidates is a direct result of several important social changes that have occurred over the past half-century, many of which were enumerated in Chapter 2. During that time, cities lost many qualified people simply because they moved out of the city. Other potential candidates have refused to run because of the increasing personal and financial disclosures required of those running for public office. They simply do not want their entire lives thrown into the public spotlight. Some people choose not to run because of the large number of meetings one has to attend during the campaign, the sheer number of people one has to solicit for support and the sharply negative personal assaults one must endure from the opponent and the opponent's supporters.

Still others, because urban systems are media centers and public officials are under constant press scrutiny, find the very public nature of being an elected official unattractive. Public scrutiny, managing the access and reporting of the press and receiving demands from constituents of varying and often narrow viewpoints are all common reasons some people reject running for public office, particularly school board.

Ironically, public and media attention can often discourage qualified candidates, but tends to attract less-desirable candidates to run for office. Such people have not earned enough money to worry about financial disclosure laws, and they enjoy basking in media attention because they have not received much recognition elsewhere in their lives. For them, running for school board provides a wonderful venue for gaining the public exposure they desire. They see it as a way to advance their own agendas and help them possibly move on to higher office, which in turn further enhances their public standing. Neither of these personal ambitions is helpful to the education of our children or to the effective management of a large public education system.

Others may run for school board because they have a specific agenda they want to pursue. They may run because they don't like the superintendent, they don't want a particular school closed, they support or oppose charter schools or a particular curriculum, or any variety of other school components. When I ran for office, one of the other candidates was running to eliminate soda vending machines in the schools. That was her primary policy goal, if elected. Removing soda vending machines from schools was not necessarily a bad idea, but being a single-issue activist did not necessarily qualify her for a position on the school board.

When asked to review candidates for school board in my own city, I have found that they can usually be sorted into one of three categories: social activists, single-issue advocates or union loyalists. Not that there is anything wrong with any of these groups; they simply are not obviously the best-qualified people to govern our schools. Their membership on a school board also makes for a volatile mixture of special interests. They have trouble agreeing on a common strategy, and often they simply don't like one another.

Public school systems, particularly those in urban areas, are large, complex organizations. They need wonderfully qualified people who have the competency to plan strategically, to hire effective leaders and to set policy. In most cases, the people who now run for school board, particularly in urban areas, do not possess those skills.

In early 2005, I asked two leading figures in education (who, because of their respective positions, traveled extensively to urban school systems throughout the country) whether they could name one urban school district that had an effectively operating school board. They both shook their heads and said, "No!" They both found that unqualified people serving on school boards was pervasive. Now that might have just been the situation at that time, but my own research suggests that well-functioning school boards are rare, and, even when they do exist, they do not last.

Effective leadership, at the school board level, has nearly become impossible in urban public school systems. Unqualified people cannot develop effective long-term plans for the improvement of schools. Qualified people, when they do bravely run and get elected, cannot install any sustainable changes because within two years (i.e., by the next election), their new colleagues may not agree on the direction the previous board took and will work to develop a new direction. This situation occurs in nearly every large city, and, as a consequence, it has prevented long-term sustainable change. Thus, our largest public school systems continually perform at substandard levels, or, perhaps more accurately, they tend to perform as they have always performed—poorly.

The constant upheaval of school board membership combined with the fact that usually some members are poorly qualified or unqualified, creates massive turnover in superintendents. Quite often the school district's overarching strategy is the plan of the superintendent and has been endorsed by the current school board. However, if the board's makeup changes, the new members may not want to follow the current plan. Since the plan was likely developed by the existing superintendent, the new members will aim toward hiring a new superintendent. This rapid turnover scenario occurs with great regularity. It has gotten so bad that the Council of Great City Schools (an organization representing the nation's largest school districts) reports that urban superintendents have an average tenure of only 3.64 years.[100] This is up from 2.33 years in 1999.[101] It seems that at any given time, at least 20 percent to 25 percent of America's 100 largest school systems are in search of a new superintendent.

It is nearly impossible for anyone to make major changes in a large organization in just two or three years. A leader can get started, but that is insufficient time to make a large organization into a more effective functioning enterprise. Even if a leader can be effective in a short time, as was the case in Seattle, the progress is short lived. Changing priorities of school boards cause systems to jump from one plan to another, with the ultimate outcome being no meaningful change at all.

---

100. "Council of Great City Schools," *Urban Indicator* (Fall 2010), 2.
101. Ibid.

Moreover, as was pointed out earlier, there are generally few competent superintendent candidates for boards to evaluate. Thus, a superintendent who has been fired from one school district will often end up being hired by another district. This parade of mediocrity continues until retirement.

Incompetent school board members and a revolving door of superintendents is a recipe for disaster. That is exactly what we have in most urban public school systems and will continue to have until we either change the manner by which school boards are selected or change the governance model for school districts.

Because of the problems described above, some cities have replaced elected school boards with appointed boards. In most cases, this has occurred when the state legislature has taken over an urban system. The cause of such a takeover is the conclusion, by the legislature, that the city's schools were beyond repair and were unlikely to improve under the existing governance model. Generally, when this occurs, the mayor is given control over the schools and over the selection of the school board. This has been the case in Cleveland, Boston, New York City, Washington, D.C., Chicago and Baltimore. In some cases, the mayor also selected the superintendent.

This trend toward appointed school boards is an appropriate change in the governance of urban public education systems. Though it is too early to tell whether appointed school boards are better able to institute sustainable change, it is obvious that such a process is likely to yield more qualified board members than the present elected system. If a city has an outstanding mayor, he or she is likely to appoint outstanding school board members. It is even unlikely that a very poor mayor would appoint incompetent people to the local school board. Mayors, after all, are more visible to the public—and more accountable.

Perhaps an even more radical idea is to eliminate urban school boards entirely. Under this concept, the superintendent would be part of the mayor's cabinet just like the heads of city departments. The superintendent would be accountable to the mayor. A mayor hiring a truly gifted superintendent to lead without a school board would create a school district governance structure that is effective, efficient and responsive both to the community and to the teaching staff of the public schools. Though this at first sounds as if it would eliminate local control, it might do just the opposite. A well-run school system would be a great asset to any city. Excellent schools attract families and businesses, and both help make cities more livable for everyone. Most mayors understand this and would work hard to ensure their city had a well-managed and well-functioning school system. The one caveat to this idea is that it requires that the mayor have available a selection of outstanding leaders for the superintendent position. Unfortunately, we don't have that situation now, but could have if the recommendations of Chapter 6 are implemented.

As an example of an effective school system with appointed leadership, look to the universities. With few exceptions, all major public universities have appointed trustees or regents. These appointees are carefully selected and bring a lifetime of relevant experience to their positions. My alma mater is the University of Washington in Seattle. The state governor appoints the regents for this university. Becoming a regent is a great honor, and only the most successful and outstanding citizens are appointed to the position. I cannot imagine how the University of Washington would have achieved its present world-class status if its regents had been popularly elected.

Unless and until qualified candidates choose to run for school board positions (particularly in urban school systems), our students will be better served by an appointed board or no board at all. To improve the quality of urban educational systems, all major cities should at least move to the appointed form of school governance. This would require a change in state law, enabled by a shared outlook of both the legislature and the governor. It would take political courage, which is in short supply these days, but it is nonetheless the right thing to do. The current governance model for urban, and some suburban, school districts simply does not work.

The education of our children is too important to leave to amateurs, local activists and political junkies. If school boards are retained, then we need to have the best and brightest people serving on them. Improving public education requires an improved governance model, one free of the weaknesses described above. Eliminating the elected school board, particularly for urban school systems, is an idea worth trying since the present form of governance is clearly not working.

Part Three:
Next Steps

8.

GROUP VERSUS

INDIVIDUALIZED LEARNING

A PARENT NEEDS TO HAVE ONLY TWO CHILDREN TO KNOW HOW TO-tally different children can be. However, America's educational system is set up to educate groups of students rather than each student. The assumption is that group-based learning can be both effective and economical. The results dispute both assumptions.

Bell-shaped Curve

IN THE early years of the twentieth century, schools operated on the notion of the bell-shaped curve. The thinking was that in any given class there would be smart students, average students and dumb students. Within a classroom of 25 or so students, teachers were expected to grade students using a bell-shaped curve. In other words, within that classroom, there would two or three "A" students, four or five "B" students, eight to ten "C" students, four or five "D" students and two or three "F" students. Teachers who gave a disproportionate number of "A's" or "F's" were chastised for faulty grading instead of being either complimented or assessed for the quality of their teaching. Much of this bell-curve thinking still exists in our public school system. Many teachers still expect only a few of their students to achieve "A" performance, and it is usually assumed that at least some students will not be able to achieve passing-level work. This outdated thinking is both statistically and educationally unsound.

It is statistically unsound, because, as any student of statistics will point out, a group of 25 is too small to provide a normal distribution curve, so even if the idea were to make educational sense, it does not make statistical sense.

It is educationally unsound because it is exclusively based upon a supposed normal distribution of intelligence. However, in human behavior, intelligence is only one factor in a person's ability to learn and perform. Other factors, such as motivation, self-discipline, effort or access (exposure to learning), may have as much or more influence on a child's ability to learn. "In one study of U.S. eighth graders, it was found that the best predictor of academic performance was not the children's IQ scores—but their self-discipline."[102] Moreover, if the purpose of a public school is to educate all children, then it is ridiculous to assume, at the outset, that some children will not or cannot learn.

The bell-curve structure also sets up a select-and-sort system of education. The idea is to find out who are the smartest students and who are not so smart, rather than focusing on making sure every child is learning. Our public schools were set up, and to a large degree still are today, like a swimming meet rather than a swimming lesson. In a swimming meet, the purpose is to determine who is the fastest swimmer. In public schools we spend a lot of time grading students on what they have learned and then ranking them, rather than ensuring that every child has learned. What we need, however, is a public school system that is organized like a swimming lesson. In a swimming lesson, the instructor's goal is different. The goal is to make sure all students, even the slowest, learn how to swim. Swimming meets can be a result of swimming lessons, and grading can be a result of learning, but ranking students by ability should not be the primary goal of teachers or of the system as a whole.

In swimming, as in any other athletic or artistic endeavor, classes are grouped based upon the current ability of the students, not based on age.

---

102. Amanda Ripley, *The Smartest Kids in the World* (New York: Simon and Schuster, 2013), 120.

A swimming coach would never consider putting advanced swimmers and beginning swimmers in the same class, even if they were the same age. Similarly, a music teacher would not put an advanced piano player in a class with beginners. It just doesn't make sense. Age is not a relevant factor in either swimming or piano lessons, but it is the overriding factor in our schools. No other major learning activity is strictly aged-based. Our schools shouldn't be either.

Curriculum

THIS SAME bell-curve thinking permeates the curriculum. To this day, textbook publishers develop textbooks designed to meet the expected average capabilities of children of a specific age. Third-grade textbooks are designed for the average eight-year-old child, as determined by a group of educators. Students in the third grade, for example, are given a curriculum based upon the average third-grade student, regardless of the learning readiness of the students in that class. The result is that some students become bored, because they are far more advanced than the presumed third-grade average, and some students become frustrated, because they are one or more years behind in their learning and are unable to keep up. In a class of 25 students, it is possible to have 20 who are below grade level and one or two who are two or three years above grade level. A teacher trying to teach a third-grade curriculum to such a class often ends up as frustrated as the students.

Testing

TESTING IS another area in which our public education system uses group-based measurements rather than looking at individual performance. Most academic tests, whether given at the local level or applied nationally, tend to measure a student's performance compared to that of other students. "Above the national average" is a term many school districts use to evaluate their students' performance. However, being above average really does not tell the student or the parents what the student knows and is able to do. Is the national average itself at a good level or merely a mediocre level? Who knows? Is an "A" grade given in Mrs. Wilson's class superior performance or just above average? Who knows?

Grading this way tells us which students are achieving within a particular classroom, but does not give us a clear indication of learning. Some teachers grade hard, others easy. Some high schools have high academic standards; others do not. Universities know that grade inflation has run amuck in this country. They know that a 4.0 grade-point average from one high school may bear little resemblance to a 4.0 grade-point average from another. In fact, it is a well-known fact that certain high schools receive many more university acceptances than do others. Thus, where children attend high school, as opposed to their true academic achievement, can determine whether they will receive a college acceptance.

In all of these instances, the issue of learning is subordinated to the issue of ranking. Knowing who had the best test scores or who learned the fastest is not the correct measure. What we need to measure is whether every child learned. By changing our system to focus on the learning of the individual child, we will begin ensuring that every child learns. We will also ensure that every child, upon graduation from high school, will be ready for college or for the world of work.

The problems I described are exacerbated as students grow older. By the time students are in high school, if their learning needs have not been met in the early school years, they are likely to become so frustrated and demoralized that they drop out. Others continue, just to get by, and will graduate from high school barely able to read their own diploma. It is a crisis both for our young people and for our country, as we continue to fail to educate millions of our citizens, who are then unable to earn a decent living in our society and whose children will likely start school ill-prepared to learn. It is a vicious cycle. This under-education of our citizens is one of the main reasons we are seeing an increase in poverty and stubbornly high unemployment numbers. A recent study by the Opportunity Nation coalition, found that, "6 million Americans, aged

16–24, are neither in school nor working." The coalition also found that, "in 49 states, the number of families living in poverty has increased and in 45 states, household median incomes has fallen in the last year."[103]

The report goes on to note: "the nation's largest cities Chicago, Houston, Dallas, Miami, Philadelphia, New York, Los Angeles, Atlanta and Riverside, California, have more than 100,000 idle youth."[104]

These young people are very likely to live their adult lives in poverty, many will be incarcerated, and most will be dependent upon welfare, instead of becoming productive citizens who pay taxes.

The above situation is the result of our failure to effectively educate our young people. Failure to deal with the learning needs of an individual children at the point where they are in their learning is a recipe for failure. We have been doing that for decades.

This group-versus-individual schooling not only fails to serve those who are behind in their learning, it fails to serve a lot of very bright children who suffer from ADHD or similar maladies. These children are often some of our smartest young people, but they are not wired to receive and process information in the same way most of us do. When a school or district has only have one type of learning system, these children are also poorly served. This becomes another educational tragedy for the children, their parents and our society.

Tracking

ANOTHER ASPECT of group-based education is tracking. This often starts early in a child's education and is based on teacher evaluations of a student's ability to learn. Students who are behind are put on a slower track and are given a less-demanding curriculum. Once on a slow track, a student is unlikely ever to catch up. This situation causes millions of students to receive an inadequate education, one that fails to prepare them for the society in which they will live. Tracking is an outgrowth of the bell-curve thinking of the past and is still with us today.

103. "Not in School and Not Working," *Education News* (October 25, 2013), 2.
104. Ibid., 3.

Tracking also occurs because of a propensity for teachers to have low expectations for certain children. Children from minority communities, children raised in poverty, children whose native language is not English, all regularly encounter teachers who expect them to perform below the level of other children. Once this occurs, it becomes a self-fulfilling prophecy.

Many minority children and many children raised in poverty are very likely to start school behind in their learning, and, if their delay is not corrected quickly, they will continue to fall behind. In fact, they will fall further behind as each year passes. However, being behind in learning is no indication of an inability to learn. All children, regardless of background or race (unless they are mentally handicapped), have the capacity to learn. We just need to ensure they are given the right opportunity to do so.

Conclusion

TODAY, BECAUSE of the failure of our education system, we now have almost three generations of adults who are poorly educated or under-educated for the demands of the world in which they live. These people are often high school dropouts, often are people of color, and often live in poverty. Not only are these adults not prepared for the world of work, but they are not equipped to be the kinds of parents who properly prepare their children for school. We can't blame them, but we can prevent their children from experiencing the same fate.

Suffice to say, all children are different, and all children have different learning needs, different learning interests, different learning readiness. A group-based learning system will never effectively educate all our children. Moving the system from focusing on groups to focusing on the learning needs of individual children will be a big step in ensuring the effective education of every child. One of the fastest ways to make this shift is through the advent of technology and its increasing use in the classroom. We will discuss this issue in Chapter 10.

9.

A Longer Day/Year and Time versus Achievement

The idea of a longer school day and a longer school year has validity only if we have corrected the other problems in the system. Discussing a longer school day and longer school year before we address teaching, leadership and governance problems would simply provide our children with a longer but still lousy school year. But, if we make the changes to improve teaching quality, school leadership and education governance, then a longer school day and a longer school year make all kinds of sense, at least for some children.

Longer Day and Longer Year

As stated before, America has the shortest academic year in the developed world. That makes no sense when we all know our children need to be educated to a much higher level today than at any time in our history. It is unreasonable to assume that our kids can learn the same amount of material in 180 days that a Korean child will learn in 220 days. We have smart children, but our short school year handicaps them.

It is even more unreasonable to assume that a child who enters kindergarten one to two years behind other children is going to catch up by going to school the same length of time as a well-prepared child. Not only do such children need much more exposure to education, but it is also quite likely that going home after school could, in fact, be detrimental to their learning. Many children come from home environments where education is not stressed and where learning opportunities are minimal. Having such students stay at school longer can be doubly productive to their growth and development.

Recognizing that all our children need to learn more today than ever before, we should extend the academic year for everyone. A simple change would be to extend the school day to seven hours (it is currently six hours or less) and to extend the school year to 205 days (from the current 178 or so days). If we did that, our children would spend 33 percent more time in the classroom. That adds up to four more years of schooling over a twelve-year educational period. I have no doubt our children would learn more and would be better equipped for post-secondary learning, if we simply lengthened our current school calendar (again assuming that we have qualified people in both the classroom and the principal's office).

The longer day and the longer year would also help eliminate the pressing need for remedial education for those who attend college. Currently, almost half the students who attend either a four-year or two-year post-secondary school need remediation in at least one subject. This is an enormous waste of time and resources, and it adds to an already costly effort by students to obtain an advanced education.

As mentioned earlier, the longer day and the longer year would help eliminate the current feeling that teachers are underpaid. Extending the day and year, without changing the hourly rate of compensation, would substantially increase the yearly salary of every teacher.

Finally, the longer day and the longer year would help eliminate the achievement gap (the difference in performance between many minority children and both white and Asian children), and it would reduce, if not eliminate, the dropout problem we now face. This latter point will be explained below.

A longer school day and longer school year may not be necessary for every student. Students who are fast learners or those who come to school extraordinarily well-prepared may not even need to attend school as long as our current school year. However, we have many children who would benefit greatly from having more time to achieve the learning goals we set for them and to gain the skills and knowledge they will need to be productive adults.

Time versus Achievement

DURING ONE of my visits to Texas, I heard a principal set the issue out very succinctly. He said:

> In the equation of education, time is the constant and achievement is the variable. What we need is to have achievement be the constant and, by definition, time becomes the variable.

A 180-degree shift! A paradigm shift!

Moving to an achievement-based system of learning would force a complete change in how we organize the school day and the school year, and would even change how the classroom is operated. It would also require a shift in the culture of our society. The summer break, for some students, would not take place in mid-June, but would fall later—and more briefly—in the summer.

In an achievement-based system, schools would be organized by achievement groups or levels, with class size determined by the current level of learning of the students, not by their ages. The less prepared a student, the smaller would be the class size and the more individualized the instruction. Less-prepared students would attend school for a longer day and for a longer year, until they reached a standard of learning appropriate for students of their approximate age. Only when they had learned what was required would they move on to higher levels. A good analogy to this type of educational system is the merit badge system used by the Boy Scouts. In Scouting, a young person can become an Eagle Scout at any age between 10 and 18. However, no Scout can earn Eagle rank without achieving the satisfactory completion of all the merit badges required. We thus have Eagle Scouts of varying ages, but none has failed to meet the standard.

Achievement grouping is not tracking or ability grouping, and it should not be confused with this kind of traditional grouping. Tracking and ability grouping set a student on a certain path based on the assumption that the student is either a gifted or a mediocre learner. Once on a track, the student would either be made college-ready or be given a lower level of learning designed to accommodate their abilities as assessed by others.

In an achievement-based system, it is assumed that all children can achieve at a high level. The system simply recognizes that some children have had more access to knowledge and learning than others and that some children can learn certain subjects faster than others.

Levels Not Grades

An achievement-based system would not have grades one, two, three and so on, nor would it have letter grades A, B and C. Students would start the year by being placed in appropriate levels and would remain there until they had met the standard of learning for that level. Children behind in their learning would be put in smaller classes with gifted teachers to speed up their pace of learning. Then they would move to the next level, regardless of whether or not the month of June had happened to arrive.

For example, today a student takes Algebra I for a year, regardless of whether the child requires six weeks or 26 weeks to learn the material. The student is then graded on their performance relative to other students in the class. The grade is based on a standard of performance established by the teacher, the school or the District office. A student may receive an "A" or some lesser grade based on performance. The focus in our current system is on sorting and teaching, not learning. All students receive the same material, presented in the same manner, and students are graded on how well they absorbed the lessons presented. The focus is also on time.

In an achievement-based system, the math student would move on to Algebra II once they had mastered Algebra I, regardless of the time required. Such a system focuses on student learning, not teaching and sorting, and it has the advantage of not being constrained by time or age.

In an achievement-based system, children would be placed in levels based not on age but on their current level of learning. Achievement grouping would put students into classrooms in which all the students would be at approximately the same level of learning, regardless of age. By doing this we would allow each child to keep moving forward in his or her learning and children would not be placed with a classroom group that is either years ahead or far behind where they are in their own learning. For example, if a kindergartner is already reading, but not doing well in math, that child may attend class at level two or three for reading, but would go to class at level one for math.

Students who start school well behind in their learning would be put in smaller classes, with individualized instruction, while those at or above standard in their learning would be put in more advanced classes that may well have a larger number of students. By making this shift, students who are behind in their learning would get more assistance so they could catch up, and those who are advanced in their learning would not be held back. Each type of student would be allowed to learn at his or her own pace, and would not be constrained in their advancement. Also, we would use teachers' time more effectively, thereby enhancing their ability to teach and increase their job satisfaction.

Those students who need more work would attend school longer each day and perhaps more days each year. This increased school time would be provided to mitigate age differences and to ensure that every child learns. Under this system, no one would be left behind, no one would fail academically, and students would not move up until they had learned what they needed to learn.

Built into this thinking is the philosophy that all children can learn, learn, but some need more time than others. If you don't believe that, then a longer day/year would be absurd. However, if you do believe it (as I do), then it is incumbent upon us to create an environment in which that learning can occur and to recognize that every child's learning occurs in different ways and at different times and at a different pace. The assumption is also that the child is exposed to effective teaching. This latter point will minimize the time a child needs to learn material, as effective teaching has been shown to greatly enhance the pace of learning. Also, not all children would have to learn to advanced levels in various subjects, but all would be required to learn what is deemed necessary in order to be a responsible citizen.

This flexible system would accommodate the five-year-old child who has been blessed with a loving and nurturing home, who has been exposed to books since infancy, who has been on a computer for three years, who know numbers and is reading at an elementary level by the time that child arrives for the first day of kindergarten. It would also accommodate the five-year-old child who has never experienced a stable home environment, never been exposed to books, who has never seen a computer, and who may not speak English. In our present system, these two students could be assigned to the same classroom, with the same curriculum, delivered the same way for the same length of time, and we would expect them to achieve the same learning outcome. This rigid approach has never worked and it will never work. It's insane!

Creating an achievement-based system will also require a societal change. We could have 12-year-olds graduating from high school and older students getting personalized attention and attending school for a longer day and year. The former could be mitigated by bringing college-level courses into the high school as is now done with Advanced Placement courses and International Baccalaureate courses. If this were to be done, it could dramatically reduce the cost of college for many families. Students who graduated early might be able to achieve one or two years of college education without ever having paid tuition. This is already occurring through another program called Running Start, which allows advanced high school students to take classes at community colleges or universities. The one disadvantage of this program is that the student has to leave high school and attend classes at the community college or university. Either idea achieves the same goal, but bringing college courses into the high school would be far more convenient, potentially less disruptive and probably less expensive for the state. It would also keep students in buildings with students of similar age and social development.

For those students who are behind in their learning, even at the high school level, they would be put in small classes with gifted teachers and may well stay in school longer each year. These students would receive extensive remediation to ensure they learned and to prevent dramatically extending their high school beyond the time of other students.

Regardless of how we cater to advanced learners, a standard high school diploma would no longer automatically represent the four-year learning experience. Instead high school would last as long as it took for the student to achieve standard in all academic subjects and mature in their total development. Such a system would focus on the needs of the individual student and would work to ensure that students achieved at their highest level. Moreover, students would not be permitted to fail. Students would move as fast as their ability and motivation would allow. Frustration, both for the student and for the teacher, would be minimized and student learning would be maximized. Also, if children know, at the outset, that they will remain in school until they achieve a defined academic standard, they will have great motivation to engage themselves in learning. Having to attend school while their friends enjoy the summer holiday would be a huge incentive to learn the material.

In *The Poisoned Apple*, Betty Wallace points out that achievement grouping is a preferred educational system in three fundamental ways:

> First, it holds high standards for all students, not just some. It assumes that progress up the achievement staircase is more a function of

effort than intelligence. It assumes that all students are smart enough to reach the top. No one is locked into lower levels.

Achievement grouping also is fluid. It does not force students to move from one level to the next in whole groups. A student can advance whenever he is ready, whether it takes him three or thirteen months.

Finally, students in achievement groups are not judged on the basis of how they compare to others of the same age. Instead, they are evaluated on what they know and are able to do and compared against a standard of performance. When they meet the standard at one level, they move to the next. There are no losers. Everyone who tries; advances.

Public Schools must shift to more fluid structures and individualized instruction if they are ever to succeed in preparing all, or even most, students to be effective adults in the modern world.... The uniform, age-based U.S. public education system does not fit the nation's increasingly diverse culture.[105]

There are other elements to an achievement-level structure that make it worth attempting. First, by assessing the learning readiness of each child, it will be possible to have larger classes for some teachers, since the teacher is instructing only students who are already at or above the standard for a given level. Conversely, students who are behind in their learning would be placed in small classes where they would receive constant individualized instruction. In both cases, money would be saved because we would be more efficient in the employment of teachers and we would have fewer dropouts, thereby improving students' future earnings potential. As we know, educating our children effectively would reduce the need for many of today's social services. A well-educated citizen requires less government support and contributes more in taxes.

Obviously, schools with high percentages of children from poverty or English language learners would need more teachers and smaller classes. These students would also need a longer school day and a longer

105. Betty Wallace and William Graves, *The Poisoned Apple* (New York: St. Martin's Press, 1995), 23–24.

school year. This would obviously be more expensive and would require increased public funding to support it. However, this system would reduce the dropout rate, which would add revenues to a district. Schools and those districts with well-prepared students could operate with larger classes and reduced payrolls. In both cases, money saved from increased efficiency could be made available to fund the students who need it the most.

The concept of eliminating both grade levels and letter grades is already occurring in several school districts. "A version of the technique has been adopted by at least 29 small districts, organizations and schools nationwide. Results show that students taught with the method are up to 55 percent more likely to pass state standardized tests."[106]

A research report in 2010, by the Colorado-based Marzano Research Laboratory, showed that: "schools that use the model are 37 percent more likely to score proficient or above on state tests for reading, 54 percent more likely to score proficient or above on state tests for writing and 55 percent more likely to score proficient or above on state tests for mathematics than schools that did not use the model."[107]

Standards

AN ACHIEVEMENT-BASED system could work only if standards of achievement were in place. Standards of achievement for the core academic skills would need to be established for each level. With standards and the expectation that every child will learn, the need for selecting and sorting is eliminated. A student would be at standard, below standard or above standard. We would not need to know that Sally is smarter than David, or that Paul learns the material faster than Michelle. We would need to know only that each student has mastered the subject before being advanced to the next level.

---

106. "Michigan Initiative Scraps Grade Levels and Letter Grades," *Education Week* (October 3, 2012), 12.
107. Ibid., 12.

The creation of standards is currently taking place with the adoption of the Common Core, a set of standards that has been developed by education leaders in many states. It is a voluntary set of standards that is being widely adopted throughout the country. Common Core comprises standards for English/language arts and math that could form the basis of an achievement-based system.

The Common Core standards are not without controversy. Several states have decided not to adopt them. Some people feel they are too hard; others feel they are too easy. Still others are concerned that they are just another government mandate. Regardless of what becomes of the Common Core, standards of some sort are needed so we can assess the level of education being provided and acquired by our children.

In many circles within the education community, the Common Core adoption is seen as the key to improving our schools. That is a misled assumption. Standards will not improve schools, but they will help assess school effectiveness.

Establishing good standards and trying to impose them on a failed system is like a failing business developing a new budget and expecting that to change the way the business performs, even though a stronger budget may well be needed. A poorly performing business needs a lot more than a new budget to change its performance, and our schools need a lot more than standards. Right now, we have the "cart before the horse."

This point does not negate the validity of the standards; it just makes it unlikely standards will have any major impact until we fix our failed system of public education. Also, since the Common Core only deals with English/language arts and math, it is a very limited start on the development of standards. However, even if we develop standards for other courses, such as geography, biology, etc., we should not lose sight of the need to educate our children in areas that are beyond the traditional academic core. For example, all children should take a course in economics so they understand how our economy works. They should take a course on civics to grasp the structure and function of government. They should take courses in the liberal arts, ancient and recent history, etc. Standards for these can be developed and will be needed. However, not every subject needs a standard. The arts, such as music, drama, etc., don't need a standard, but are still very worthwhile to learn. As discussed in Chapter 3, the "total development" of a child encompasses much more than instructing our children in the core academic subjects.

Conclusion

TREATING ALL children the same, as we mostly do now in our current education system, does not recognize how different we all are from one another. Our education system needs to cater to those differences. As Thomas Jefferson said, "The highest form of discrimination is to treat unequal people equally." We do that every day in every school and it must stop.

Extending the school day and the school year, and moving to an achievement-based system of education, would be a major change not only for our schools, but also for our society. It would force almost everything we know and think about our schools to change. Not only would students, parents and educators have to change their view of school, but also our entire society would have to look at education differently. Some children would have to attend school well into the summer in order to meet academic standards and be ready to move on. The impact on families, educators and businesses (such as the travel and tourism industries) would be immense. It is, however, the only way for us to be serious about effectively educating every child. If that is what this nation wants and needs, then we must focus first on the needs of our children and not let ourselves get diverted by the needs and wants of adults.

If we implement these changes, and do it right, then over the next decade we will see a change in the learning readiness of our children. As each level of learning occurs, fewer and fewer children would be behind in their learning. As that occurs, more and more children would move with their peers and age-level differences would be mitigated. Fewer and fewer children would need specialized help, the dropout rate would diminish and the need for the longer school day and school year would be reduced. As in Finland, children would take charge of their learning and their level of academic success would dramatically increase. At that point, the goal of effectively educating every child in every school would be achieved.

10.

TECHNOLOGY

THE COMPUTER AND INTERNET HAVE GIVEN US THE INFORMATION Age—with still unrealized potential for education. Children, at an early age, are being exposed to interconnected computers and digital tablets with which they can play games or engage in authentic learning— and they can do this at any time they desire and at almost any location. A student in central Africa can access the Library of Congress. A child in central China can speak directly and visually with a child in Minnesota. There are no barriers, no constraints on information flow and no limits on the potential acquisition of knowledge.

But schools have been among the slowest segments of our society to respond to the advantages of technology. Many years ago, someone said to me that, "It only took 45 years for the overhead projector to move from the bowling ally to the classroom." That comment may not be totally accurate, but it does reflect the slowness of schools to adopt new technologies.

The primary reason schools are so slow to adapt to change is the lack of training provided to our teachers. If teachers are not taught to use a view graph, they are unlikely to feel a need to do so. The same is true for computers. Schools buy things that are going to be used in the classroom, so, if teachers do not use computers, then districts tend not to buy them. This is not always true, as some districts have spent millions on technological acquisitions, only to find they are not being effectively implemented. Also, as Alexander Russo, a highly regarded commentator on education change, has written, "most schools are wired, but few have school-wide Wi-Fi or enough bandwidth to allow everyone to be connected at the same time."[108]

Today, most children start using computers at a very early age. Middle- and upper-class families are raising children skilled in using digital technology. Even in homes of poverty, children are often exposed to cable TV and smart phones. However, there is still very limited employment of technology in America's classrooms. The primary reason, again, rests with the ability of the teacher to effectively employ new devices and the competency of school district administrators to support them.

I don't mean to imply that technology is not being used in public education. It certainly is. We now have high-tech schools, where technology pervades every aspect of student learning. We also see computers being used in almost every school. As a system, however, technology has not revolutionized learning as it has most other endeavors. That is slowly changing as new products and services are being developed on a daily basis for implementation into our education system.

Today there are products and services for teacher training, for curriculum and instruction, for testing and assessment, for tracking student progress and for the financial management of schools and districts. New companies are constantly being formed to develop tools to enhance education methods in some way. In addition, there are the social media platforms, particularly YouTube, that provide video content that may be immediately relevant to a current classroom project.

However, we have not yet seen the technology breakthrough in education that has occurred almost everywhere else in our society, but it will come. As Lillian Pace, senior sirector of national policy for knowledge works, states:

> Over the next decade, our education system will experience the kind of deep disruption and reconfiguration that Amazon, iTunes and Zipcar brought to their respective industries. The concept of "school" will take many forms where learning is no longer defined by time and

---

108. Alexander Russo, "Notable Education Stories," *The Atlantic* (December 5, 2013), 6.

place. Radical personalization will become the norm as learners and families create individualized learning "playlists" and educators embrace new roles ...[109]

Technology is a game changer. It has the capacity to change fundamentally how learning takes place, how teaching is provided, and how assessments are performed.

New technology can also be very expensive, can be poorly employed or have little or no good effect on students. For example, today, we are seeing technology being implemented almost like a new fad. Recently, Los Angeles schools decided to provide an iPad to every student. Other districts have done similar things, but not on the same scale. The Los Angeles effort has been fraught with problems: "There have been questions about the exact cost of individual devices, students' demonstrated ability to circumvent the security filters on the tools—and questions about the readiness of curriculum developed by Pearson that is designed to be embedded in the devices."[110]

Obviously, the effective implementation of technology requires a lot more than just purchasing a new computer or mobile device. Wireless Internet systems have to be in place and functional throughout all buildings, support services need to be readily available, teachers need to be trained in how to use the devices, and the relevant curriculum needs to be reviewed, approved and installed on the devices. Students need to understand their own responsibility, particularly when it comes to portable devices. If one is lost or broken, who has to pay? What if a student forgets to bring the device to class?

All of these issues have already shown up in the Los Angeles implementation. After spending over $500 million to purchase iPads, the *Los Angeles Times* reported, the "Board of Education held a special meet-

109. Lillian Pace, "A Pathway for the Future of Education," *Education Week* (September 25, 2013), 32.

110. Sean Cavanagh, "District Officials Eye Blended Learning, With Cautionary Lessons in Mind," *Education Week Online* (November 5, 2013), http://www.edweek.org/ew/articles/2013/11/06/11techtrends.h33.html.

ing to discuss these and other issues and ultimately slowed the rollout that began with 47 campuses."[111] On August 27, 2014, the Los Angeles School District terminated this entire program. The *Los Angeles Times* indicated that it had been a "total failure."

Like so many reform efforts of the past, new ideas become accepted as the latest "key" to improving our schools. Major effort and money are plowed into the new system only to find out that the costly change made little or no difference. Technology implementation is no exception. We know that the degree to which something is successful is dependent upon the skill and effort of those involved and the amount of planning and scheduling that is done prior to implementation.

Training

EMPLOYING TECHNOLOGY effectively for student learning depends upon the degree to which our teachers are skilled in the use of technology and in their ability to employ it as a teaching tool. It also requires high-quality curriculum to be available online and full support of the system. When that occurs, effective learning will occur, whether the child is in the classroom or located in some distance place.

Most new teachers have grown up with technology, so they should already be comfortable in using a computer. Usually what they need is to be trained on what new technology to use and how to use it. Unfortunately, most schools of education are not staffed with professors who have great competence in technology and its employment in learning. Until that changes, our new teachers are unlikely to come into the profession ready to employ relevant technology.

The fastest way to get technology training for our new teachers would be to employ professors from a university's school of computer science to work with the school of education. That is unlikely to occur, but it would be a good idea. For now, our schools will have to hope that

---

111. Howard Blume, "Mixed Reaction to iPad Rollout From L.A. Teachers and Administrators," *Los Angeles Times* (December 2, 2013), http://www.latimes.com/local/la-me-ipads-survey-20131202-story.html.

new teachers have learned how to use technology on their own. Teachers who have been in the profession for many years are likely to need extensive training in the use of technology.

Massive Open Online Courses (MOOC)

PERHAPS THE largest use of technology in learning has occurred with Massive Open Online Courses or MOOCs. These are educational courses that are open to anyone and can be accessed via the Internet from almost anywhere. Perhaps the most well known of MOOCs is Coursera, an online service started at Stanford University. It is now a separate organization offering over 500 courses for free. After less than two years of operation, Coursera has reached almost 5.4 million students worldwide.[112]

Most MOOCs are offered by colleges, but they have started to permeate the K–12 sector as well. Employed primarily in high school courses, these online courses can allow students to study courses not available at their own school, can supplement the information provided in their current classroom, or can be treated as a core course of the school.

The most stellar example is the Khan Academy, a nonprofit formed by one individual inventor, Sol Khan. Khan develops video courses on numerous subjects and then makes them available to anyone in the world. Today, there are "6 million unique users clicking on Khan Academy videos (mostly made by Sol Khan himself) each month.... It is a worldwide phenomenon."[113] Students from all over the world are tuning in to learn from one teacher, Sol Khan. Today, there are "4,120-plus videos posted on the site. They are available in 216 countries, in more than 30,000 classrooms, as well as countless more linking in from home or elsewhere."[114] Khan's videos are being translated into many languages, which increases the global reach of his educational work.

---

112. http://www.coursera.org.
113. "Sal Khan Is A Can-do Guy," *The Costco Connection* (August, 2013), 30.
114. Ibid., 32.

MOOCs provide the opportunity for a single gifted teacher to reach thousands of students, thereby enhancing their effectiveness and dramatically reducing the cost to the students or to the government.

Many school districts are starting to employ MOOCs. Like anything new, the roll-out is not without difficulty or problems. Determining when and how to test students is still being worked out, as are concerns about cheating. Determining the role, if any, for parents is still being discussed. Nonetheless, MOOCs will likely see increasing deployment in K–12 schools.

Students will likely find it attractive to have flexibility about when and where they engage in coursework. They will be able to repeat lectures or lessons over and over again until they fully understand the material. Teachers will be able to reduce their time on presentation and have more time to work directly with students, thereby increasing the individualization of learning. Principals and district administrators will enjoy the increased effectiveness of teachers as well as the decrease in costs.

Teacher Preparation

EMPLOYING TECHNOLOGY in the training of teachers is as valuable as its use in the education of K–12 students. Allowing teachers to see and speak with some of our country's most effective teachers will provide would-be teachers with additional insights into their chosen vocation. Videos of gifted teachers applying their craft with real students provide an excellent training opportunity for new teachers. Being able to see different ways of teaching the same subject is also possible with technology. Live chats with the instructor in the video can now occur, thereby increasing the value of video observations.

Technology will also change the way teachers teach. They will have to change their pedagogy from teacher-centered to student-centered. Since students will have access to the same information that is available to the teacher, it will necessitate that the teacher serve as more of a coach than a "sage on a stage."

Learning how to employ technology in the classroom should now become an important component of teacher preparation. Understanding how to employ technology to enhance student learning, to assess student progress and to determine student needs will greatly increase the effectiveness of tomorrow's teachers.

Technology will not diminish the role of the teacher, but rather re-design it.

Curriculum

TECHNOLOGY IS quickly making textbooks obsolete. Publishers are putting their textbooks on discs or even making them available via the online "cloud." In either case, the student is rid of heavy books and can access any material immediately and the publisher can update the texts on an on-going basis. Also, with iPads or computers, students can access the material from anywhere at any time.

There is a revolution going on with regard to curriculum. Courses in all subjects are now being made available to parents and students alike via the computer. In addition, material is presented in different ways in order to meet the different learning needs of individual students. The traditional method of one teacher presenting material to a group of students for a specific length of class time and then moving on to another subject is now no longer viable. The one-size-fits-all model is going away fast. Students need not fall behind, because they can view a video or listen to a lecture as many times as needed. Computer technology truly individualizes learning. Students can sit in a chair, lie on the floor, talk, work with friends or use any other means necessary to understand the material. They can also do it on their own time.

Assessment

WITH NEW technology, assessing student learning is easier than in the past. Systems are now in place that allows a teacher to assess the learning level of each student and to provide students with help on an as-needed basis. With real-time data, teachers can ensure that every child is learning. Immediate assistance can be provided at the very time the child needs help.

Testing is also easier with technology. Many online courses now come with assessment systems built into the course. In many cases, there is continuous assessment so the student cannot move to the next portion of a course until he or she has demonstrated knowledge of prior material. This built-in assessment not only ensures that learning takes place, but negates the need to have end-of-course tests or high-stakes testing, because the student's level of learning is already known by the time he or she has completed a given course of study.

This is much different from today's testing regimen. As Tony Wagner points out in *The Global Achievement Gap*: "Our current accountability system primarily tests how much students have memorized and can recall at a given moment in time, and there are fifty different state standards for what it means to be proficient—none of which meet the standards for work, college or citizenship in the twenty-first century."[115]

Obviously, we need a different and better student assessment system. By incorporating continuous testing as a student moves through material, it will be possible to ensure learning and eliminate the high-stakes testing that has become the norm in our schools today. Employing technology as an integral part of all educational curriculum will make that possible.

Student Preparation

FOR MIDDLE- and upper-class families, computers are integral to their way of living. Young children in those families are using computer devices from a very early age. These children come to school already comfortable with electronic devices and almost dependent upon them.

However, we also have a large percentage of students who may well enter kindergarten without ever having seen a computer, let alone having knowledge of how to use it. These children are far behind their peers

---

115. Tony Wagner, *The Global Achievement Gap* (New York: Basic Books, 2008), 125.

in the use of new technology and in their own readiness to learn. Again, these children will need a smaller class, more individualized attention and specific instruction on using technology, and a longer school day and school year before they can catch up with their peers.

Conclusion

TECHNOLOGY WILL revolutionize learning as it has already revolutionized most of our society. Learning will become a 24/7 activity and school will be where students go for further clarification of information, for in-depth study of material, for hands-on learning such as a chemistry lab or problem-solving in a math class, for music, art and athletic participation and for social interaction with their peers. School will be a place where students go to learn how to think critically and communicate effectively.

This is particularly exciting for those students who are behind in their learning, who have a poor learning environment at home, and who may well have little access to technology at home. These kids will be the greatest beneficiaries of new technology in schools, because they will be able to work at their own pace, will be able to go over material again and again until they understand it, will be able to skip over material they already know and will have access to quality instruction in every subject. Examples of this are already being seen in dozens, if not hundreds, of schools across the nation.

For example, education researcher Liv Finne describes KIPP Empower: "This elementary school in South Los Angeles uses digital technology to deliver small group instruction to groups of 14 kindergarten students and 19 first-grade students. In 2010–11, the percentage of KIPP Empower students reading at 'proficient' or 'advanced' levels increased from 36 percent to 96 percent."[116]

Other similar successes are being seen in both public and private schools across the country. These successes are proving that digital

---

116. Liv Finne, "Review of Digital Leaning in Private Schools and Public Charter Schools," Washington Policy Center (November 3, 2013), http://www.washingtonpolicy.org/publications/notes/review-digital-learning-private-schools-and-public-charter-schools.

learning methods can improve the academic achievement of all students, can enhance the effectiveness and attractiveness of the teaching profession and can reduce the cost of providing a good education.

We are seeing that curriculum, testing and teaching methods are all changing. In fact, change will become the norm, just as it has become the norm in other parts of our lives. As we know, many of the jobs our children will perform in the future do not even exist today. Thus, we need students who have learned how to learn, know how to think critically and know how to communicate effectively. With great teachers and the effective use of technology, we will be able to teach all children those skills and prepare them for life in the twenty-first century.

11.

CHOICE, VOUCHERS AND CHARTERS

ALL OF US HAVE, AT ONE TIME OR ANOTHER, BEEN TOLD THAT THE solution to fixing our public schools is to have choice in our selection of schools, to have vouchers that would allow us to go to any school we wanted or to have charter schools available.

All are good ideas, but I do not believe any of them, by themselves, are the solution.

School Choice

WHEN I was on the school board in Seattle, we took a serious look at our student assignment policies. These were the policies that determined where a child would attend school. The existing policies were based upon a geographical boundary around each school. If parents lived within that boundary, their child would attend that specific school. If they lived near a quality school, they were happy with the system. If they lived near a lower-quality school, they were not. This system gave the decision to the district, not the parents, regarding the school their child would attend. We decided that we needed to make a change to give our parents more say in the selection of their child's school. As we delved into the issue it became apparent that we could not achieve an optimum solution.

In urban systems, where there are many schools within a reasonable distance of any home, the idea of choice would seem to make a lot of sense. However, one needs to recognize that many people select the neighborhood in which they live, based upon their assessment of the nearby school. Parents who make that choice are adamant about wanting to attend their neighborhood school—as well they should be. They exercised their choice when they selected the house to buy or apartment to rent. However, those who live in a neighborhood where their school is not up to the standard they would like are equally adamant that they have a choice of where to send their child to school. They, too, have a valid argument. So how can one satisfy both views? Basically, one can't!

In student assignment issues, one finds that if you maximize choice, you minimize predictability. If you maximize predictability, you minimize choice. It is a dilemma that all urban school boards and district leaders face.

It is primarily an urban issue because most suburban and rural school systems do not have the concentration of people or schools to make choice a valid option. Transportation and distances make it unpalatable for most districts. However, often people move to suburbs because of the school system, so they have already enjoyed and exercised their choice.

So we come back to the urban school dilemma. As long as schools vary widely in quality, this issue will be with us. Thus, the best solution is simply to make every school a quality school and then choice becomes much less critical. I believe we can get there but, in the meantime, it is appropriate to take a look at how to create a system of assignment that has some fairness to it.

After much debate, my school board colleagues and I determined that the best student assignment solution would be to have a limited choice option with a preference to the neighborhood school. Under this system, those who wanted predictability could retain it, but those who wanted other options could also have them, although to a limited extent.

That is the policy we developed for the parents of Seattle and it seemed to work fairly well. Because of transportation costs, we limited choice to a geographical area, but a much larger area than the boundaries of a single school. The boundaries we set up had at least four elementary schools, two middle schools and two high schools within them. Within that area, parents could send their child to any school (that had room) and be provided transportation to get that child to and from the school. The net effect was to give parents choice. It wasn't total choice, but it did give parents some options and it did force some schools to seriously look at what they needed to do to make themselves more attractive to their parent community.

Even within that system, choice turned out to be quite limited as the perceived high-quality schools would fill up with local children and thus provided relatively less choice to those outside the neighborhood. Regardless of the limitations, the new assignment system met our goals and provided options, though constrained, to our parent community.

As we debated the issue of choice and predictability, another reality surfaced. That reality had to do with capacity. Providing meaningful choice to parents will work only if the district has excess capacity in schools. If every school is filled to capacity, choice is greatly constrained. Most districts do not want and cannot afford excess capacity in their schools or to have extra schools, so choice is again restricted regardless of how desirable it might be. The impact of this fact is the recognition that some children, regardless of choice options, will be required to attend the school assigned to them by the district.

A modicum of choice also can be achieved by creating specialized schools within the public system. Schools that focus on science, music, art, international studies, etc., are quite common in many districts. Sometimes such schools are referred to as *magnet schools* and are generally open to any student in the district. These schools often are made available on a lottery basis since they are over-subscribed. Also, they are generally limited to high schools.

As you can see from the above, choice within a given district sounds like a good idea, but in practice is very difficult to achieve and of course, one is assuming here that school boards and administrators are even open to choice.

An alternative of choice in the public schools is to give parents the right to have their children attend private schools. Religious schools are often not part of this equation because of the need to "separate church and state." (I find this a fallacious argument, but it nonetheless seems to be the rule in most states.) Nonetheless, having the choice of going to a private school sounds like a good answer to the choice question. However, in reality, it often doesn't yield much choice either. Often, private schools have waiting lists, and so new entrants have limited chance of selection. Also, private schools know that certain children cost more to educate than others, and so they can and do select students based upon the perceived cost to educate. Affluent parents are also more likely to have their child selected for admission.

School Vouchers

MUCH HAS been written about vouchers as a solution to failing inner-city schools. The notion behind vouchers is to provide parents with a slip of paper or some other allocation that had a specific dollar value. This voucher would then be given to the school of their choice, and that school would receive, from the state, the value on the voucher. Basically, parents would be given the tuition money needed to send their child to a specific school. With this voucher, the argument goes, parents could select any school of their choosing and be able to finance the cost of having their child attend that school. It is another way to create choice for parents.

Again, it sounds like a great idea, but it is very hard to put into practice for the same reasons as mentioned above. High-quality schools tend to fill up with local students or, in the case of private schools, students who come from affluent families. In either case the options for the student to attend a specific school are quite limited.

The other problem with vouchers is the higher-than-average cost to educate certain children. If every child were to receive the same voucher (in terms of dollars), then schools would naturally accept the easiest to educate students. By doing so, the school would maximize their revenue and minimize their costs.

To make vouchers work, you would again need excess capacity in the school system and the vouchers would need to be weighted to reflect the differing cost to educate various children. Children who come to school well-prepared and children who are ill-prepared or who don't speak English or have some type of physical or mental impairment are all different. The under-prepared or the impaired student costs a lot more to educate. Again, referring to my time on the Seattle School Board, we effectively put in a weighted voucher system when we installed what we called the *weighted student formula.*

By weighting each student, we were able to take into account the differing costs to educate specific children. By making this adjustment, those schools with the most ill-prepared students received the most money. With the extra money, these schools were able to fund all-day kindergarten (at the elementary level) and reduce class sizes at all levels. Both outcomes increased the attractiveness of these schools to the parents they served. Smaller classes allowed for more individualized instruction, which enhanced academic achievement.

In combination with the implementation of the weighted student formula, we also put in the choice program mentioned above. The net effect was to create a free-market system inside the public system. The budgets of schools were now determined by both the *number* and the *type* of students who *chose* to attend. And, if students chose not to attend, the school was underfunded and had to reduce staff and cut expenses.

This new reality changed the way schools operated. Principals and staff members recognized that they needed to make their school attractive to parents or they would not be able to retain their jobs or remain at the school. This reality was vividly shown one evening when I attended an elementary school PTA meeting. At that meeting, staff from four middle schools (two of which were magnet schools) were making presentations to attract the students of the fifth-grade parents attending the meeting. Each school talked about its academic programs, the school culture, special programs offered, etc. It was wonderful to see. Creating competition within the public system served to improve all schools.

The schools were able to determine what types of students they wanted to attract and how much funding they needed to operate. High-revenue students (those whose students needed more time and attention to meet standards), would become increasingly attractive to schools, thereby giving their parents more choice. As schools improved their performance and as children were brought up to standard, the differences in weighing could be diminished.

Like choice, a weighted voucher could be helpful in improving schools. Both items should be part of an overall strategy of school improvement.

Charter Schools

IN RECENT years there has been a major push to pass charter laws in the various states. Today, some 42 states and the District of Columbia have enacted charter school laws. The city of New Orleans has the largest concentration of charter schools of any city in the country. This occurred as a result of hurricane Katrina and the devastation it created in the city's schools. In rebuilding that system, the state de-regulated the schools of the city and set up an organization called the Recovery School District (RSC). Almost all the schools of New Orleans were given to the RSC, and today all 70 schools of the RSC are charters. Of those that remained with the Orleans School District, 12 are operated as charters and four remain as traditional public schools. The Orleans School District continues to own all of the buildings in both their district and those in the RSC. New Orleans is the first city in the country to have over 50 percent of the students attending charter schools.[117] In Washington, D.C., 44 percent attend charter schools.[118]

Many years ago, I wrote an editorial against the passage of a charter school law in the State of Washington. My rationale for the editorial was the realization that charter schools are simply de-regulated public schools. If the de-regulation of some schools is such a great idea, why does it not make sense to de-regulate all schools? I still feel that way, even though I now support charter schools in my state. I do that because it is unlikely that my state (Washington) will anytime soon deregulate its public schools. Until it does, charter schools provide a much-needed alternative to the traditional public schools, particularly in poverty neighborhoods. They provide real choice when there is none.

In most cases, charter schools are created in neighborhoods where the schools are failing or under-performing. Sometimes, a mayor or a state education department will ask a charter organization to take over one or more failing schools. By being free of the constraints of both the state regulations and the union contract terms, charter schools can operate totally different than public schools, and in many cases perform substantially better.

In states with charter school laws, there are thousands of children being served by innovative schools that have a variety of strategies and curriculums. Some charters are one-off schools that have been established by a group of teachers, or a nonprofit group. Over the years, charter management organizations have developed that operate multiple schools. Perhaps the best-known charter management group is KIPP (Knowledge Is Power Program). KIPP schools are now in multiple states and are producing wonderful results. KIPP schools are generally grade 5–8 schools that serve low-income populations. These schools operate a longer day and a longer year. Students wear uniforms, teachers are carefully selected and trained, and the principals are also carefully selected

117. Orleans Parish Schools: http://www.nops.k12.la.us.
118. Friends of Choice in Urban Schools: http://www.focusdc.org.

and trained. In many cases, the principals are former KIPP teachers. Recently, KIPP has opened some elementary schools and is again achieving wonderful results.

In New Orleans, there are charter schools that focus on math and science, schools that focus on music and schools that focus on art. Parents have a wide array of educational options available to them, including traditional public schools. New Orleans, which used to lag the state of Louisiana in standardized test scores, is now close to the top. Graduation rates from high school rose from 54.4 percent before Katrina to 77.6 percent in 2013.[119]

Innovation and creativity is much more likely to occur in a charter school than in a traditional public school, because the staff has been carefully selected and the principal and teachers are free to do what they feel will most assist their students. In this environment, teachers have higher job satisfaction, principals have more authority, and parents have more choice. It is a win-win. De-regulating our public schools would lead to the same result. In essence, New Orleans has done that.

The best example of a state deregulating public schools has occurred recently in the State of Wisconsin. There, Governor Walker and the state legislature curtailed public employee union collective bargaining rights. This made union membership voluntary, with the result that schools could now be operated without regard to the constraints of their union contracts. As a result, schools are now operating with far more autonomy than they have ever had and teachers are able to teach as they deem necessary for the students in their care. Time will tell whether these changes positively impact student performance. My concern is that the changes were made before the state implemented the changes I suggest in Chapters 5, 6 and 7 (teacher quality, leadership improvement and improved governance). Without those changes, sustained improvement may still not occur.

---

119. New Orleans Business Alliance, "New Orleans High School Graduation Rate Outperforms U.S.," June 18, 2013, http://nolaba.org/new-orleans-high-school-grad-rate-outperforms-us/.

Conclusion

THE REALITY of our public schools is that choice, vouchers and charters can apply only to a small percentage of our schools and the students who attend them. State laws, transportation constraints, local demand and/or lack of access limit the impact that either of these ideas can have. However, if all states do what Louisiana and Wisconsin have done, then the system would be effectively de-regulated and innovative schools would be allowed to develop. These can be traditional public schools or charters—it really doesn't matter. What matters is that the school has quality teachers, effective leadership, and the autonomy to provide the best education the staff can deliver. When that occurs, students learn, regardless of their socio-economic status. Supplementing that with a weighted funding system would create a major improvement in the academic performance of our nation's children.

Until we are able to de-regulate our public schools, it makes sense to continue to push for choice, vouchers and charters. Each has the potential to improve the academic opportunity for some students, and that makes it worth doing. However, we need to recognize that the solution to our education crisis rests with improving our public schools, not coming up with ideas that merely skirt the crisis?.

12.

Brain Development and Early Childhood Education

Medical researchers have labeled the decade of the 1990s as the "Decade of the Brain." During that decade, an enormous amount of progress was made in understanding the human brain and how it develops. What was learned, along with subsequent findings, has great implications for education and for the early development of our children.

Brain Development

When you talk about education, what you are really talking about is brain development. All of us come out of the womb as insatiable learners. From the moment we take our first breath we are engaged in a remarkable learning journey, and learning is the process of developing our brain. Thus, understanding how the brain develops is critical to enhancing the learning of children.

In this generation, we are discovering more than ever before about the brain and how and when it is developed. We are also learning how brain development depends upon the exposure both to learning and to nurturing relationships. In fact, nurturing relationships are crucial to brain development.

It is estimated that the human brain (the most complex three pounds on the planet) has about 100 billion neurons or brain cells at birth.[120] "The first three years of life are a period of incredible growth in all areas of a baby's development. A newborn's brain is about 25 percent of its ultimate weight. By age 3, it has grown dramatically by producing billions of cells and hundreds of millions of connections, or synapses, between the cells."[121] This is what makes the early years so vitally important, write Doctors Bruce Perry and John Marceilus:

> During the first three-years of life, the human brain develops to 90 percent of adult size and puts in place the majority of systems and structures that will be responsible for all future emotional, behavioral, social and physiological function during the rest of life.[122]

Even in a child's initial years, some culling occurs as certain connections are used and others are not. Synaptic pruning occurs—"tuning" the brain for efficient processing. This is a time when language acquisition is important. As babies hears words, they also tune out other sounds. By age one, writes Jack P. Skonoff, the brain will no longer hear certain sounds.

> [B]y 12 months of age, the human brain can differentiate all the sounds of the spoken language(s) to which it has been exposed. As the brain goes on to develop the circuits that figure out how groups of sounds represent words that have specific meaning, it relies on those earlier circuits to distinguish one sound from another. This is often followed by the formation of circuits that make it possible to combine words into sentences and express increasingly complex thoughts over time. Thus, learning at age 2 builds on what was mastered at age 1 and, in turn, lays the continuing foundation for what will be learned at age 3 and beyond. Stated in simple terms, circuits build on circuits and skill begets skill.[123]

---

120. "Baby Brain Map," *Zero to Three*, http://www.zerotothree.org/child-development/brain-development/baby-brain-map.html.
121. Ibid.
122. Dr. Bruce Perry, "Personal Perspective: The Time Is Now," http://www.scholastic.com/teachers/article/personal-perspective-time-now.
123. Jack P. Shonkoff, "The Science of Early Childhood Development," Concept Paper for the Board of Directors of Thrive by Five (July 2006), 9.

Nurturing relationships assume distinctive significance in healthy brain development. Children start to develop powerful cognitive capabilities, complex emotions and essential social skills in the earliest years. Nurturing environments are, therefore, essential to early learning. For example, language is learned in relationships. Exposure alone does not do it. This was learned in an experiment where young babies were exposed to tapes of people talking Mandarin Chinese. A similar group of babies were held and then spoken to in Mandarin. The latter group captured the sounds of the language without difficulty. The former did not.[124]

Learning language is, therefore, both acoustical and emotional. The human element is integral to language acquisition. Early childhood language acquisition is dependent upon both hearing the words and hearing them in a nurturing setting. Unfortunately, we have lots of children who receive neither. Jack Shonkoff, professor of human development and social policy at Brandeis University, substantiates this point by pointing out that:

> Genes determine when specific brain circuits are formed and individual experiences shape how that formation unfolds. Appropriate sensory input (e.g., through hearing and vision) and stable, responsive relationships build healthy brain architecture that provides a strong foundation for learning, behavior and health. The most important relationships begin in the family, but often also involve other adults who play important roles in the lives of young children, including providers of early care and education.[125]

Such data show up in the issues we have earlier raised about the learning readiness of children raised in poverty. These children have many disadvantages that begin certainly at birth, if not before.

---

124. Patricia Kuhn, "The Linguistic Genius of Babies," *TEDxRainier* (October, 2010), http://ilabs.washington.edu/i-labs-news/dr-kuhls-ted-talk-linguistic-genius-of-babies.
125. Jack P. Shonkoff and Deborah A. Phillips, eds., *From Neurons to Neighborhoods: The Science of Early Childhood Development* (Washington, D.C.: National Academy Press, 2000), 8.

For example, in a landmark study, Hart and Risley discovered that early language acquisition is substantially different in children raised in poverty and those raised in affluence. They found that the number of words heard by a baby in one household is substantially different than in another household. This difference is vividly seen when both children start kindergarten. In a home where at least one parent is a professional, a child will hear 2,153 words per waking hour. In a working class home, the number is 1,251 words per hour. A child growing up in a welfare home averages only 616 words per hour.[126] The net effect is that over the course of one year, the welfare child will hear 3 million words and the child raised in the home of a professional will hear 11 million words. Over five years, this difference is staggering—55 million versus 15 million. The impact on IQ and school readiness is profound.

Stress is another factor that impacts children raised in poverty. In those homes, often there is only one parent and never enough money to meet the family needs, so both food and housing become stress points. This stress is felt by the baby or child and can have lasting impact on development. Long-term stress damages the brain, lowers the immune response, affects sleep, makes learning and memory harder, makes peer relationships harder and contributes to depression. "In almost every way that it can be tested, chronic stress hurts our ability to learn,"[127] reports University of Washington professor, John Medina. Obviously, long-term stress can dramatically influence the social and emotional health of a child and, therefore impact the learning readiness of any child entering school.

A child needs consistent, nurturing relationships in order to develop. Such relationships shape self-awareness, social competence, conscience, emotional growth and more—all skills needed for the "total develop-

126. Betty Hart and Todd R. Risley, "Meaningful Differences in Everyday Experience of Young American Children." See http://www.strategiesforchildren.org/researchbriefs.html.
127. John Medina, *Brain Rules: 12 Principles for Surviving and Thriving at Work, Home and School* (Seattle: Pear Press, 2008), 186.

ment" of the child. In fact, says Medina, "One of the greatest predictors of performance in school turns out to be the emotional stability of the home."[128]

Today, an increasing number of our young children are being raised in environments that do not prepare them for school or life. These children are way behind before they enter the front door of school on their first day of kindergarten. They quickly dislike school and dislike learning. Prior to their senior year they are very likely to drop out. Without massive intervention early in their schooling these children are doomed to a mediocre education and an adulthood of poverty, welfare and even incarceration.

In earlier parts of this book, we have discussed how we need to change the K–12 system, so it will work for these children. They need the longer day and year, as well as smaller class sizes. They need wonderful teachers who can convey subject matter in an interesting and engaging manner, who are nurturers, who genuinely care about these kids and who provide these children with both the love and the compassion that they often fail to get at home. Even if we were to fix our schools today, we would have at least a generation more of these unfortunate children. All of us need to understand the needs they have and we must ensure their needs are met. As long as we have children being raised in environments that don't prepare them for learning, we will have to have schools equipped to make up for the deprivation these children suffered in their early years.

Going forward, however, the better solution is to intervene earlier in the child's life.

The Case for Preschool

THERE HAVE been very few federal programs that have provided the results that were intended. One partial exception is Head Start. This program of providing preschool to under-served populations has been

---

128. Ibid., 190.

shown to positively affect young children. Obviously, not every Head Start program has been successful, but where effectively implemented with caring, nurturing providers, it has been a success.

That should not be too surprising, because the data irrefutably show that high-quality early childhood education enhances a child's performance in K–12 schooling. Numerous studies have made that case. What has not occurred, however, is the uniform availability of quality preschool for those children who most need it. Though Head Start helps, it is not sufficient to reach all the children who would benefit most from early education. Even where it is effective, it is insufficient.

At both the state and the federal levels there is now increased discussion and effort being put into early childhood education. This is a very positive development, but I fear that the outcome will not be what is needed. That fear is based on the premise that the root cause of a child's lack of preparation for learning is not the child, but rather the parents. No discussion is being provided about how we, as a society, can help these parents be better caregivers to their children, thereby raising children better prepared to learn.

John Gottman is a well-known researcher who has concentrated his work on families and early childhood development. What he has learned is that intervention with parents can dramatically improve marriages and the social and emotional development of their children. Given what Gottman has learned, John Medina has suggested that, "first grade begin a week after birth."[129] In fact, the child's learning should begin with the education of the parents.

Given what we know about the importance of the home environment to the successful development of a child, it would seem prudent for our education system and our health-care system to work together to influence our future students and citizens. It should start in the maternity ward. Hospitals and Ob/Gyn doctors should recognize a responsibility they have of counseling new parents on what they can do to assist in

---

129. Ibid., 199.

the healthy brain development of their child. These new and would-be parents need to understand their responsibilities and the fact that they are not only their child's first teacher, but their child's most important teacher.

In those instances where the parent cannot or will not provide a nurturing and loving home environment, society must pick up the slack. Early childhood education and truly effective teachers can help mitigate this problem. Family, neighbors and religious organizations can also help. Failure to do so will permanently harm the child and make the child less likely to successfully become an adult capable of living in a civilized society. In that event the cost to society is far greater (less income earned, less money paid in taxes, unhealthy living, and possible incarceration) than would have been the cost of effective early childhood intervention.

Early Childhood Education

GAIL JOSEPH, a University of Washington College of Education researcher has stated that; "There are 1825 days between the day a child is born and the day she turns five and enters kindergarten. During that time, the child is learning to be a social being. Children can learn to be aggressive, or they can learn more peaceful ways to inhabit the world."[130]

How children are raised during these early years will significantly influence the type of person they will become. Thus, it is imperative that we provide all our children with an early life that will prepare them to live in a civilized society. To do that requires that we make provisions for early childhood education for those children who will not receive it at home. We should also, as mentioned above, develop programs for the parents of these children—parents who are either under-educated adults who were failed by an ineffective school system or recent immigrants who may not have had any formal education. In either case, their

---

130. "Emotional Literacy: Rethinking Problem Behavior in Preschool," *A Fair Start: Equity and Excellence in Early Childhood Education*, in *Research that Matters* vol. 6 (Seattle: University of Washington, 2008), 5. See https://flipflashpages.uniflip.com/3/93263/331853/pub/html5.html.

children run the risk of not being properly prepared for school and life. Today, there are millions of children and an even greater number of parents who fit that description.

Quality preschool and early learning centers are desperately needed to fill this void. Efforts are underway in many states to provide universal preschool, but that is not what is needed. There are millions of children who are receiving excellent nurturing and learning at home. These children do not need a new state or federal program. However, there are many children who do need high-quality day care where they will receive emotional guidance, social stimulation and language acquisition.

Politicians and many educational activists suggest this can be done only by establishing new federal or state early childhood programs. I disagree! We have tried that with limited results and at a high cost. A better solution would be to assist existing institutions to provide this service. Organizations such as the YMCA, the Salvation Army and similar nonprofit organizations already have extensive programs serving this need. Helping churches, synagogues and temples set up preschools would also provide access for many parents. In addition to being less expensive than a state or federal program, these institutions are more likely to be staffed by nurturing adults who could provide the children with the type of environment they desperately need. Also, unlike federal or state programs, ineffective personnel can be removed and ineffective programs can be closed.

A possible way of encouraging the establishment or expansion of such programs would be to give a preschool voucher to parents living in poverty. The voucher would be designed to cover 80–90 percent of the preschool costs. By not funding all of the costs, it would ensure that parents had to put up some minimal amount of money to get their child enrolled. By having some "skin in the game," parents would be more selective and more demanding on the type of program in which they chose to enroll their child. This would provide a self-policing mechanism to ensure programs met the needs and/or requirements of the parents. It would also reduce the costs.

There also is debate going on as to whether preschools need to be licensed and staffed with licensed professionals. Certainly we need some standards for these types of facilities, as a lot of parents are not sophisticated or knowledgeable enough to know what their child needs. But I would question whether we need another bureaucracy. Developing a set of standards and then setting up a small inspection staff should be sufficient.

As for the staff, given the information mentioned earlier regarding brain development, these programs need to be staffed with caring, nurturing adults rather than teachers of content. These early years are much more about socialization than they are about education. What we need to ensure is that each child comes to school as a "socially and emotionally healthy child." Such a child will be able to learn quickly and succeed in almost any learning environment that child enters. Says Shonkoff:

> Emotional well-being and social competence provide a strong foundation for emerging cognitive abilities. Social skills, emotional health and cognitive-linguistic capacities are all important prerequisites for success in school and later in the workplace and community. Brain architecture and the immune system also interact as they mature, which influences all domains of development and health.[131]

Parents active in their church, synagogue or temple are the ideal types of people for providing the appropriate environment for social development. Also, providing these adults with an income as they provide a nurturing environment for the neighborhood children is a win-win situation. Nonprofits, such as the YMCA and others, are also staffed with similar types of people who help create the type of environment these children need.

---

131. Jack P. Shonkoff and Deborah A. Phillips, eds.., *From Neurons to Neighborhoods: The Science of Early Childhood Development* (Washington, D.C.: National Academy Press, 2000), 10.

In terms of our economy, this is also the right thing to do. The return on investment from early childhood education has been shown to be one of the best investments we can make. "In fact, long-term studies show that model preschool programs for children living in poverty can produce benefit-cost ratios of 17:1 and annualized internal rates of return of 18 percent over 35 years."[132]

The Perry Preschool Project (a longitudinal study that compares at-risk 3- and 4-year olds who attended preschool with those who did not) found that children in intensive high-quality preschool programs

- Were more likely to graduate from high-school

- Were more likely to have a job

- Had significantly higher earnings

- Had a significantly higher rate of home and car ownership and had a savings account

- Were less likely to use sedatives, sleeping pills, tranquilizers or drugs

- Had significantly fewer arrests and were less likely to be arrested for violent crimes or for property or drug crimes

- Had savings in crime costs (for example, males in the program cost the public 41 percent less in crime cost per person)[133]

Early childhood education for at-risk children is not only the right thing to provide, it is an essential element to insuring the effective education of every child. As a society, we need to look at education, not as a K–12 system, but as a program of child development that goes from birth until the child is capable of becoming a productive citizen.

---

132. Ibid., 14.
133. Lawrence J. Schweinhart, president, High/Scope Educational Research Foundation, *Lifetime Effects: The High/Scope Perry Preschool Study Through Age 40* (Ypsilanti, Mich: High/Scope Press, 2005).

13.

A CALL TO ACTION

EDUCATION IS PERHAPS THE MOST TALKED ABOUT ISSUE IN OUR SO-
ciety. We hear about education issues from parents, teachers, politicians, union leaders, business leaders and the general public. Everyone
is concerned about the education of our children, and everyone seems
to have a solution or idea of what we need to do. That is not new; it has
been discussed for decades. In fact, back in 1983, in the famous report *A
Nation at Risk*, the comment was made,

> Our once unchallenged preeminence of commerce, industry, sci-
> ence, and technological innovation is being overtaken by competition
> throughout the world.... The educational foundations of our society
> are presently being eroded by a rising tide of mediocrity that threatens
> our very future as a Nation and a people.... We have, in effect, been
> committing an act of unthinking, unilateral educational disarma-
> ment.[134]

In the intervening 30 years, the discussion has continued, but the results have been negligible. All kinds of ideas and efforts have been made
with no significant change in outcome.

Today, we are seeing major efforts being made to install the Common Core standards, to increase charter schools, to expand school choice,
to add more rigor to our schools and to increase funding. Some of these
issues are looked upon as being solutions. Others are considered needs.

---

134. U.S. National Commission on Excellence in Education, *A Nation At Risk* (Washington,
DC: National Commission on Excellence in Education, 1983), 1.

Seldom, however, is there a discussion about a fundamental change of the system and of the people who work in it. That, as I have indicated, is the real need and what should be the topic of discussion.

The increased attention to education is a direct result of recognizing how our world has changed and the implications of those changes on the learning needs of our children. Arthur Levine articulated it when he said:

> America is moving from a national, analog, industrial economy to a global, digital, information economy. The two economies differ dramatically in their expectation for schools and teachers.
>
> Industrial societies focus on common processes, epitomized by the assembly line. Our schools—products of the industrial age—rely on such processes:
>
> Schools enroll children at age 5, sort them into classes, teach them specified subjects for uniform lengths of time determined by the Carnegie Foundation for the Advancement of Teaching in 1906, and require attendance 180 days annually for 13 years.[135]

Marion Brady summarized the situation well when he stated that:

> America is no longer an industrial society, but our schools still operate with the "industrial" model. The focus is on teaching, not learning. As a consequence, American education isn't up to the challenge. The evidence is inescapable. Millions of kids walk away from school long before they're scheduled to graduate. Millions more stay but disengage. Half of those entering the teaching profession soon abandon it. Administrators play musical chairs. Barbed wire surrounds many schools, and police patrol hallways. School bond levies usually fail. Superficial fads—old ideas resurrected with new names—come and go with depressing regularity. Think tanks crank out millions of words of ignored advice, and foundations spend billions to promote seemingly sound ideas that make little or no difference. About a half-trillion dollars a year is invested in education, but most adults remember little and

---

135. Arthur Levine, "The Plight of Teachers' Unions," *Education Week* (May 8, 2013), 36.

make practical use of even less of what they once learned in thousands of hours of instruction.[136]

Brady paints a pretty bleak picture, but he is describing what many of our schools look like and what many of us experienced in our K–12 experience.

Our American culture is based on some core values such as individualism, initiative, spontaneity, and creativity. We admire the independent thinker, think personal autonomy is a very good thing, and believe every person should be helped to realize his or her full potential. But we create and continue to maintain an educational system at near-total odds with what we say we believe. Instead, we standardize. Just about every school in the country—public, private, parochial, charter, magnet, virtual, home, whatever—uses the same calendar, the same curriculum, the same or very similar standards, the same nationally distributed, interchangeable textbooks, and the same corporately produced standardized tests. The lack of public protest testifies to the inability of most to realize how at odds our values are to our approach to educating.

Every student, for example, must take higher math, this despite the fact that in any randomly selected school, it's unlikely that more than a small handful will have enough mathematical ability and interest to consider making active, productive use of it. How much sense does it make to put a math whiz in an algebra classroom with 25 or 30 aspiring lawyers, dancers, automatic transmission specialists, social workers, surgeons, artists, hairdressers and language teachers? How much sense does it make to put hundreds of thousands of kids on the street because they can't pass algebra?[137]

The problem is obvious, but the solution has evaded us for decades. Many have tried and to no avail. However, the old adage, "failure is not an option," is what needs to be our clarion call to action. We've tried adjusting the present system and that didn't work. Now we must create a new system.

---

136. Marion Brady, "What's Worth Leaning," *Information Age Publishing* (2013), vii.
137. Ibid., 19.

Changing our education system is not for the faint of heart. We need to remember that.

We are taking on a $600 billion enterprise with more than 6 million employees. The old one-room school house has been turned into a government jobs program where the number of employees has grown four times as fast as the rate of students. Public education has become a labyrinth of political, bureaucratic and union empires that depend on a captive population of students and minimal quality control.[138]

This bureaucratic empire is very resistant to change. In my efforts, I started with the idea of changing a district and learned that it would not work at that level. Granted, you can make changes at the district level, but it is impossible to make such change last. Sustainable change is not possible at the district level because of the constant change of superintendents and school boards. Leadership and governance changes are the norm in most districts, and so we must look to the state. We must look at changing the laws that now govern the present system. To do that will take political courage, something that is in short supply.

What is needed are governors and a state legislatures willing to take on the entrenched bureaucracy of both universities and unions. One state needs to step up and lead the nation in systemic change of our education system. Both Mitch Daniels of Indiana and Jeb Bush of Florida did great work on education during their respective tenures as governors. However, neither took on certification laws or governance issues, which, in my mind, is where the effort needs to start.

We must get the right people into the profession and qualified leaders leading the system before any meaningful and sustainable change is likely to occur at either the school or district level. To do that, we must start with the certification laws, increase the qualifications for those allowed to enter the profession and develop selective and effective lead-

---

138. Jeb Bush, "Speech to the National Education Summit," *Foundation for Excellence in Education* (October 17, 2013). See http://excelined.org/downloads/remarks-by-governor-jeb-bush-at-2013-national-summit-on-education-reform_october-17-2013/.

ership training for both principals and superintendents. Then we must make changes in the governance model of our districts.

By eliminating certification laws and modifying the governance structure, particularly in urban systems, we can begin the process of upgrading the talent and competence of the people who enter the system. We can begin the process of selecting well-trained leaders in our schools and managing our districts. We could have qualified people serving on school boards (if we continue to have them) who bring a lifetime of wisdom to the effective operation of the system. We would also make working in the system far more attractive.

Many good teachers agree that dramatic reforms are needed:

> A transformed profession would give teachers much more responsibility and flexibility to make decisions that meet their students' educational needs—allowing access to and training with technology, shifting class sizes, and restructuring the school day so that they have time to collaborate with colleagues and engage in professional learning and problem solving.
>
> We would offer teachers a professional salary and career pathways that acknowledge their skill and commitment in one of the most complex, demanding and important jobs in the world. We would insist on great school leaders, with principals who have high expectations; develop all teachers as lifelong learners; and create positive school cultures where students and teachers succeed.[139]

All this might seem like a pipe dream, but it is already happening in many schools in this country. Tony Wagner, in his excellent book *The Global Achievement Gap*, describes a wonderful charter school located outside Boston. Called the Francis Parker Charter Essential School, this school has 365 students in grades 7–12 and serves a diverse student body, with more than 20 percent of the students classified as special-needs kids.

---

139. Geneviève DiBose, Claire Jellinek, et al, "Teachers Want to Lead Their Profession's Transformation," *Education Week* (February 8, 2012). See http://www.edweek.org/ew/articles/2012/02/08/20debose.h31.html.

At Francis Parker they operate with a modified level program. Kids who would be in either seventh or eight grade are in Division I. Ninth- and tenth-graders are in Division II and the eleventh- and twelfth-graders are in Division III.

> [A]ll classes are two hours in length, are interdisciplinary, and are taught by teams of two teachers in what the school calls its two Domains: Arts and Humanities; and Math Science, and Technology. All students must also take Spanish and Wellness.[140]

This particular school graduates 100 percent of its students, all of whom are accepted to college and 85 *percent graduate from college.*[141]

Still another successful innovation is being spearheaded by the Haberman Foundation out of Houston, Texas. This foundation is working on a variety of school reforms. They have initiated a program called Fast Break. It is an innovative approach to remaking high school.

- Instructors co-teach and fully integrate the teaching of reading, math, communications (oral and written), computer applications and career selection and employability skills. They also provide placement and follow-up services.

- All 2–4 instructors with different specialties stay with the same group of 25-60 students for most/all of the instructional day, modeling the kinds of teamwork and collaboration seen in the best companies.

- Concentrated, 5–8 hours a day for 8–12 weeks program provides sufficient time on task to produce good learning habits and prevent forgetting.

- Courseware, online testing and small-group instruction facilitate teaching students of different ability levels at the same time.

- Highly engaging curriculum is experiential, team-oriented, and project-based, and it integrates soft skills such as teamwork, cus-

---

140. Tony Wagner, *The Global Achievement Gap* (New York: Basic Books, 2008), 243.
141. Ibid., 242.

tomer service, time management and conflict resolution into the teaching of academic skills.

- There are no bells and annoying interruptions during the school day.

- Students who meet Fast Break's Achievement, Attendance and Attitudinal requirements (the "3 A's") are rewarded with assistance in obtaining an outcome they value, such as a career entry job, college admission, or accelerated academic credit leading to the next grade-level promotion or enrollment in advanced academic or technical training.[142]

These are examples of some of the wonderful ideas starting to be implemented in high schools. The KIPP program, mentioned earlier, has some equally impressive programs for middle-school students and is now achieving similar results at the elementary level.

In each case, what is occurring is that talented people are being given the opportunity to innovate and to create exciting and effective learning environments for students. This could happen nationwide, if we simply put the right people in the right jobs and reduced regulatory constraints. Even the constraints of union contracts can be overcome with the right kind of leadership.

If we did that, we could create schools like those described by the Center on Reinventing Public Education:

> In order for schools to succeed, they need to have a clear and commonly understood definition of a graduate's character and skill set. They need to be able to develop a team of people who agree on a common plan for achieving those goals. They need a fierce determination to solve problems at home or at school that might interfere with learning. They need to set and enforce norms about learning and behavior that all adults and students agree on. They need to be able to use time

---

142. Barry E. Stern, "ACT Study Shows Little Progress in Preparing High School Graduates for College and Careers," *Education News* (September 17, 2010). See http://www.educationnews.org/ed_reports/99898.html.

and money in ways that make sense for their school and their students. And they need to be responsive to parents and accountable for results.[143]

The Broad Foundation, in awarding the Broad Prize for Charter Schools to Uncommon Schools (a charter management organization), described their schools this way: "Uncommon Schools all share key attributes: a college-preparatory mission, high standards for academics and character, a highly structured learning environment, a longer school day and a longer school year, a focus on accountability and data-driven instruction, and a faculty of committed and talented leaders and teachers."[144]

It is obvious we know what is needed. What we need is to make it a reality.

We also need to remember that all children need not go to college, but they all need to be educated. Today, welders and plumbers need to know geometry and some chemistry. Kids not planning on college need to have other career opportunities exposed to them, while still in high school. In my day, we had wood shop and metal shop as well as mechanical drawing. Today, we probably need an electrical shop, plumbing shop, computer-aided design shop, computer hardware shop, etc.

Back in the early 1990s I participated in the creation of the Thomas Jefferson School for Science and Technology that was created as an applications-only public high school in Fairfax County, Virginia. This high school, which was enormously successful from the very beginning, is still a sought-after school today. At TJS, we created several labs for the students to have hands-on engagement in specific work areas of interest. The labs included a biotechnology lab, a telecommunications lab, an applied materials lab, a computer science lab, and several others. Today, that same school has twelve such labs available to the students. Though

---

143. "Good Governance Starts and Ends with Strong Schools," *Center for Reinventing Public Education Blog* (September 17, 2013). See http://www.crpe.org/thelens/good-governance-starts-and-ends-strong-schools.

144. "Uncommon Schools Wins Broad Prize for Charter Schools," *Broad Foundation* (July 2, 2013). See http://www.broadprize.org/news/661.html.

the students in this high school were all being prepared for college, the labs were wonderful learning areas for any student interested in those particular disciplines. Similar labs could become part of high schools as we move further into the twenty-first century. Such labs could be easily staffed with talented people if we eliminated certification laws and allowed experts from specific disciplines to work in our schools.

Preparing our children either for the world of work or advanced education is a primary responsibility of the present generation of adults. Educating our children should be our highest priority, and we should have our brightest people engaged in that endeavor. We should also make sure those bright people have the freedom to innovate and the incentive to perform. They need to be well led and well governed.

So here's a condensed game plan for a governor and state legislature to enact:

1. Eliminate the monopolies in the system.
   - Eliminate certification laws to terminate the monopoly that these laws give to education schools.
   - Eliminate mandatory union membership requirements that give unions a monopoly control over personnel.
2. Upgrade the people entering the system.
   - Dramatically increase the admission requirements for education schools.
   - Develop highly selective leadership training institutes to provide our schools with talented principals and superintendents.
3. Improve governance by going to appointed school boards in urban systems or eliminating boards entirely and having superintendents report directly to the mayor.
4. For children being raised in poverty, provide subsidized funding for pre-school programs at non-profits and religious organizations.

5. Reduce state regulations governing schools and then get out of the way and let talented people engage with parents to provide the education our children need and deserve.

We know what works to make *every school* effective and we have the tools to make it happen. The big question is, "Do we have the will?"

A.

SEATTLE'S UNION CONTRACT TABLE OF CONTENTS

TABLE OF CONTENTS: 2010–2013 SPS/SEA COLLECTIVE BARGAINING AGREEMENT

ARTICLE III: GENERAL RIGHTS AND RESPONSIBILITIES

SECTION A: Administrative Responsibility and Authority

SECTION B: Nondiscrimination Rights

SECTION C: Representation Rights and Due Process

SECTION D: Employee Personnel Files

SECTION E: Academic Freedom

SECTION F: Classroom Control

SECTION G: Employee Protection

SECTION H: Safety and Security

SECTION I: No Reprisal for Disclosing Misdeeds

ARTICLE IV: PROVISIONS FOR COMPENSATION AND WORK HOURS

SECTION A: Basic Employment Contracts & Employee Responsibilities

SECTION B: Types of Employee Contracts

SECTION C: Basis for TRI and Basic Salary

SECTION D: Time Responsibility and Incentive

SECTION E: Supplemental Contracts for Stipended Assignments

SECTION F: Salary Schedule Placement

SECTION G: Miscellaneous Salary Provisions

SECTION H: Traffic Education

ARTICLE V: SUBSTITUTES

ARTICLE VI: LEAVE RULES, REGULATIONS AND PROCEDURES

SECTION A: Short Term Compensated and Uncompensated Leaves and Sabbaticals

SECTION B: Long Term Uncompensated Leaves

SECTION C: Leave for SEA Officers

ARTICLE VII: EMPLOYEE BENEFITS & PROTECTION

SECTION A: Group Insurance Provisions

SECTION B: Liability Coverage and Hold Harmless Provisions

SECTION C: Protection of Employees, Students and Property

SECTION D: Travel Allowances

SECTION E: Transportation of Students.

SECTION F: Tax Sheltered Annuities

SECTION G: Transit Passes

ARTICLE VIII: STAFFING–QUALIFICATIONS-BASED HIRING FOR CERTIFICATED NON-SUPERVISORY EMPLOYEES

SECTION A: Staffing Decisions

SECTION B: Three-Phase Staffing Process

SECTION C: Site-Based Hiring Process

SECTION D: Hiring Process for Certificated Non-Supervisory Personnel Other Than Teachers

SECTION E: Mid-year Transfers

SECTION F: Administrative Transfer Procedures

SECTION G: Special Staffing Issues at Schools Requiring SPS Intervention

SECTION H: Program Movement or Closure

SECTION I: Employees Covered Under Section 504 of the Rehabilitation Act of 1973

SECTION J: Affirmative Action

ARTICLE IX: WORKDAY, WORKLOAD, ASSIGNMENT AND SCHEDULING OF EMPLOYEES

SECTION A: Length of Workday

SECTION B: Employee Load

SECTION C: Preparation-Conference-Planning Time

SECTION D: Class Size & Staffing Ratios

SECTION E: Elementary Specialists

SECTION F: Special Education Staffing Ratios, Relief and Workload Issues

SECTION G: Covering Classes and Substitute Rebate and Reimbursement

SECTION H: School Facilities, Teaching Stations & Itinerant Workspace

SECTION I: Kindergarten Instruction

SECTION J: Bilingual Education

SECTION K: School Counselors & Social Workers

SECTION L: Student Services

SECTION M: School Libraries

SECTION N: World Languages

SECTION O: School Nurses

SECTION P: Elementary and K–8 Collaboration Time

ARTICLE X: GRIEVANCE PROVISIONS

ARTICLE XIII: NO-STRIKE CLAUSE

APPENDICES

INDEX

Made in the USA
Charleston, SC
27 September 2014